Cookie Swap!

By Lauren Chattman

WORKMAN PUBLISHING · NEW YORK

For my daughters and their many cookie-loving friends
at Sag Harbor Elementary School and Pierson Middle School

Library of Congress Cataloging-in-Publication Data is available.
ISBN 978-0-7611-5677-2

Workman books are available at special discounts when purchased in bulk for premiums
and sales promotions as well as for fund-raising or educational use. Special editions or book
excerpts also can be created to specification. For details, contact the Special Sales Director
at the address below, or send an e-mail to specialmarkets@workman.com.

Cover and interior design by Rae Ann Spitzenberger
All original photography of baked goods by Ben Fink
Food stylists: Cynthia Garcia-Vegas and Jose Martin Vegas
Prop stylist: Sara Abalan
Photo director: Anne Kerman
Author photograph on page viii by Eve Bishop
Author photograph on back cover by Jane Gill
All other photography from Fotolia

Workman Publishing Company, Inc.
225 Varick Street
New York, NY 10014-4381

www.workman.com

Printed in the United States of America
First printing September 2010

10 9 8 7 6 5 4 3 2 1

Very Vanilla Sprinkle Cookies, p. 49

Table of Contents

Everything you need to know to get your swap on, from planning and inviting to post-party recipe sharing.

Plus . . . *Happy Swap Day!* • *Cookie Swap Math* • *Excuses, Excuses: Every Day's a Swap Day* • *Gimme More: A Note on Yields* • *You're Invited . . .* • *Company Is Coming* • *Sample Swap Invitation* • *Cookie Swap Checklist* • *Kickin' It Old School: The Traditional Christmas Swap* • *Swapping Made Simple* • *Contain Yourself: Serving Pieces and Totes* • *Thanks for the Memories* • *Everything Just So: The Control Freak's Cookie Swap*

So you're ready to get baking—now gather your gear. Find tips on ingredients and equipment, and discover the genius of parchment paper.

Plus . . . *Lighten Up: Testing Your Leavening* • *Cookie Swapper's Pantry* • *The Bentley of Bittersweet: Premium Chocolate Chips* • *A Cocoa Coda: Chocolate for Every Purpose* • *Equipment Essentials* • *The Scoop on Scoops* • *Stuck on You: A Parchment Paper Love Song* • *Fresh Is Best*

All your favorites with a cookie swap twist, including Classic Oatmeal Raisin Cookies, Double Peanut Butter Cups, and the perfect chocolate chip cookies—with four unique variations (Hazelnut Espresso Chip Cookies, anyone?).

Plus . . . *A Win-Win: Chocolate Chip Cookie Bake-Off!* • *Sugar Crash: Chocolate Chip Cookie Emergencies* • *Seeds of Change: How to Seed Jam* • *Fall for Fall: Autumn Harvest Cookie Swap* • *Cinnamon Paradiso: Cookie Swap al Italia*

Nut-and-Jam Thumbprints, p. 43

Ganache-Glazed Brownie Bites, p. 57

Cardamom Palmiers, p. 86

Green Tea Cookies with Almond Cream, p. 114

Rolled Vanilla Cookies with Royal Icing, p. 136

Almond and Olive Biscotti, p. 176

Milk Chocolate-Coconut Shortbread, p. 134

CHAPTER 12 — 187
EASY PEASY
Shortcut Cookies

Put away your oven mitts—you won't need 'em here. Take it easy with gooey, luscious, almost homemade treats like Chocolate-Toffee Shortbread Fingers, No-Bake Chocolate Bourbon Bites, and Cheater's Petits Fours.

Plus . . . *The Need for Speed: Low-Commitment Cookie Swap* ⁕ *Smooth Talk: Foolproof Caramel Prep* ⁕ *Wherefore Art Thou, Petits Fours? A Brief History* ⁕ *Blue-Ribbon Bounty: Award-Worthy Swag*

Chocolate-Toffee Shortbread Fingers, p. 189

CHAPTER 13 — 204
BEYOND MILK
Perfect Swap Sips

When the crowd's thirsty for more than milk, you'll have what to serve them: drinks like Old-Fashioned Lemonade, Mulled Cider, Mini Strawberry Milk Shakes, and more.

Plus . . . *I Want Candy: Setting Up a Bonbon Buffet* ⁕ *Menu: Autumn Nibbles* ⁕ *Menu: Lemonade Stand Lunch* ⁕ *Menu: Southern Hospitality* ⁕ *Menu: Spicy Snacks for Drinks with a Kick* ⁕ *Menu: Simple Tapas*

"The Best Cookies Ever"

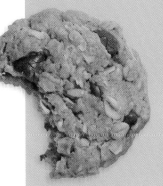

Last summer, my older daughter came home from sleepaway camp with a story that reminded me of my own days in the cabins of Camp Point CounterPoint. It wasn't about building a bonfire or short-sheeting a bed—it involved a care package, something my bunk mates and I often received from our moms and grandmas, who couldn't stand the idea of us surviving on the

jar of saltines that our rather austere dining hall director kept on a counter for between-meal snacks. In my daughter's case, the parcel came from her bunk mate's grandmother, and contained luscious bar cookies called "Seven Layers of Heaven." The grandmother had urged the girl to share the cookies with her

friends, and the group reached a near-frenzy as they dove into the treats during a rest period party. As my daughter related the story, she became rapturous all over again: "So good! The best cookies ever! I'm going to get the recipe!"

I didn't take it personally, even though my daughter was practically weaned on my home-baked cookies, and she's sampled my own seven-layer Midsummer Night's Dream Bars (page 68) several times. As a dedicated cookie swapper, professionally trained pastry chef, and cookbook author, I'm constantly developing new cookie recipes. (There's no such thing as a dessert-free day in my kitchen!) But I understood my daughter's excitement for those summer camp treats: All sweets—especially cookies—taste better when they're shared with friends.

There's no better way to enjoy the cookie-friend combo than with a cookie swap. It's a party that brings people together, to trade stories, nibbles, and recipes—and to let their hair down a little. But more important, it's a party that celebrates this most perfectly portable of desserts. What better vehicle for sugar, butter, eggs, flour?

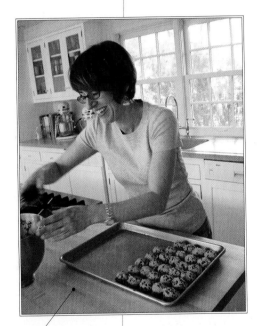

Yours truly, preparing to freeze a batch of cookies for a neighbor's swap.

A few basic ingredients lend themselves to so many possible iterations—a world of flavors and textures—all small enough to be held in the hand, a portable hug. Folks are passionate about their cookies and the recipes that are handed from parent to child, from friend to friend. So it's no wonder that when people gather to exchange their most beloved cookies, they often gush, like my daughter did, that they've just tasted the new "best cookie ever."

This, at least, is what happened to me at my first swap. I had joined a moms' group in my small town, hoping to make some friends for myself and my kids, and was later invited to the group's holiday exchange. I'm still grateful to the women who organized the event and invited me to participate, because it not only helped me make new friends, it also opened my eyes to all the wonderful baking going on around me. (Turns out I wasn't the only baking fanatic in the village!) And I walked away with a recipe for Chewy Gingersnaps (page 47) that is still one of my all-time favorites. Since then I've swapped cookies many, many times, at birthday parties, beach barbecues, preschool fund-raisers, and candidate's meetings.

I've hosted cookie swaps with a purpose, and others just for fun. Cookie swaps are the best type of potluck, because even people with no kitchen experience at all can participate. There's an element of surprise, too, and that's what always keeps it fresh.

EASY DOES IT

I know that the idea of hosting a swap can seem daunting—the planning, the math, the baking—but here's the thing: It really couldn't be easier. As baking goes, cookies are pretty low-stress; and as parties go, cookie swaps are meant to be fun, freewheeling affairs (after all, you're having a party and your guests are bringing the food!). But in case you have any lingering anxieties, I'm here to help.

In this guide I've outlined all the basics for organizing a swap, and included a handy checklist to help you plan, so you'll know exactly what to do—no guesswork necessary. And I've given you lots of road-tested party ideas and themes to get you excited and on your way. As for what to bake, you're covered there, too. I developed more than sixty easy, swap-ready recipes (plus more than thirty-five variations) for delicious, surprising cookies of all

stripes, including drop cookies, icebox cookies, bar cookies, even no-bake cookies and cookies for people with dietary restrictions.

All of the recipes bake up sizable batches—perfect for swapping—and many can be prepped in advance (these are ID'd with a "Freeze Me!" icon). And the cookies pack up and tote well—in other words, they'll hold up to any swap antics you throw their way. Beyond that, I let taste and imagination be my guide. You'll find my best versions of tempting classics like chocolate chip (page 32), oatmeal (page 45), and gingersnap cookies (page 47), and plenty of creative treats and variations like Hazelnut Espresso Chip Cookies (page 33), Double Peanut Butter Cups (page 42), and Green Tea Cookies with Almond Cream (page 114). The best part: These cookies are delectable to eat and, to varying degrees, simple to make. No matter what you bake, your swap table will be a thing of splendor—and you *won't* have to spend hours with a pastry bag in hand.

So pick an occasion (or not), whip up some cookies, and get swapping! You'll see it's as easy as pie . . . er, cookie.

Indecisive? At a swap, you don't have to choose—take plenty of each.

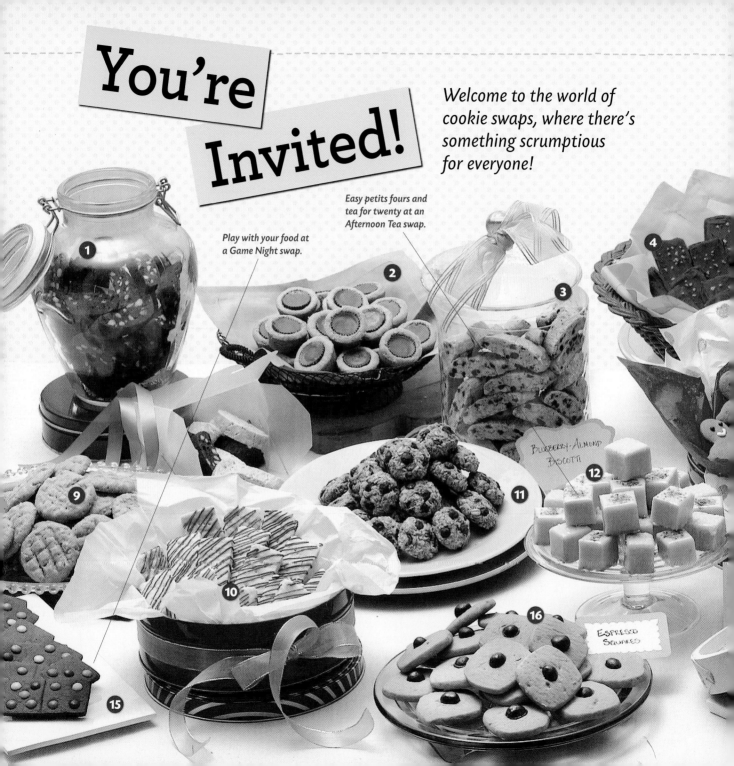

You're Invited!

Welcome to the world of cookie swaps, where there's something scrumptious for everyone!

Easy petits fours and tea for twenty at an Afternoon Tea swap.

Play with your food at a Game Night swap.

BLUEBERRY-ALMOND BISCOTTI

ESPRESSO SQUARES

Well-dressed Gingerbread Men are welcome at any holiday party.

Cute as a button—perfect for a Baby Shower swap.

Swap cookies and spread the love at a Valentine's Day mixer.

PISTACHIO SACRISTANS

5

6

7

8

13

14

17

18

Rock October with "pretzels" and beer at an Oktoberfest swap.

Brightly colored toteables liven up the table.

Shower a blushing bride with this elegant variation on Oatmeal Raisin cookies.

Ring in Halloween with a Ghouls' Night Out swap.

20

19

21

ILLA RETZELS

26

25

27

SPELT FLOUR BROWNIES

CRANBERRY-ORANGE OATMEAL

33

32

34

Savory animal crackers go wild at a Jungle Boogie swap.

Fall for fall flavors at a Thanksgiving Harvest swap.

Springtime? Swap cookies to celebrate.

22

23

24

White Chocolate & Marmalade Vanilla Wafers

CLASSIC N BARS

28

29

30

31

35

36

Photo Key

Cookie Swap!

Chapter 1

READY, SET, SWAP!

COOKIE EXCHANGE 101

Anxious to get swapping but don't know where to start? Begin at the beginning, of course. Here are all the basics—including swap math (it's simple, really) and a party-planning primer—to get you from point A to point C(ookie Swap).

HAPPY SWAP DAY!

Once upon a time, cookie swaps were strictly Christmastime affairs. They originated in the early 1900s, as a way for women to cut down on their holiday baking load—and have some fun in the process. Holiday exchanges are still wildly popular, but that doesn't mean you can't think outside of the gingerbread-and-candy-cane box. Cookie swaps are blank-canvas parties: They lend themselves to all sorts of themes and occasions. They're ideal for celebrating everything from graduations to bridal showers, and for making a silly excuse—it's Hug an Australian Day!—to gather all your favorite people in the same place. They also make excellent collaborative fund-raisers and meet-and-greets for PTAs, gardening clubs, Mommy and Me groups, pickup roller derby teams . . . whatever your cause. You can throw a cookie swap whenever you want and for any old reason—your imagination's the limit.

COOKIE SWAP MATH

After you've chosen the what and why of your cookie exchange, you need to figure out the how—and that means doing some calculations. If it's

EXCUSES, EXCUSES   EVERY DAY'S A SWAP DAY

Need a reason to have a cookie swap? Look to the calendar for inspiration, or go online to see what wacky "holidays" are celebrated at any given time. With a little creativity virtually any red-letter day can become the perfect day for a cookie swap.

For Tradition's Sake: New Year's Day, Chinese New Year, St. Patrick's Day, Mardi Gras, Easter, Mother's Day, Memorial Day, Flag Day, Father's Day, Fourth of July, Bastille Day, Labor Day, Grandparents Day, Halloween, Thanksgiving, Hanukkah, Christmas, Kwanzaa.

The Unusual and Outlandish: Inauguration Day, Rubber Ducky Day, Groundhog Day, Fat Tuesday, April Fool's Day, Spring Equinox, Secretary's Day, Kentucky Derby, Summer Solstice, National Pink Day, Friendship Day, Fall Equinox, Talk Like a Pirate Day, Oktoberfest, Black Friday. (For a longer list of out-of-the-ordinary celebrations, check out www.dailyholidays.net/)

been a while since your high school math class, you might squirm at the idea of number crunching. But in this case it couldn't be simpler. You want to determine how many people to invite, and how many cookies each person should take home with them.

First, assess your party space and draw up a guest list. If your swap will take place in your home, or in another fairly intimate space (this is assuming, of course, you don't live at Versailles), it's probably best to limit your list to a number your room can hold comfortably, say between ten

and twelve. If you're thinking big, as in a backyard, school cafeteria, or community center, then the more the merrier.

Next, determine how many cookies you'd like everyone to have when all is said and done. Let common sense be your guide. For a group with tame appetites, three or four dozen might do. A group with eager bellies or large crowds to feed might require as many as six or seven (or even eight or nine) dozen.

A common misunderstanding about the cookie swap is that the more

GIMME MORE :: A NOTE ON YIELDS

It's up to the host (that's you!) to decide how many cookies each swapper should bring. For the sake of consistency and convenience, all of the recipes in this book have yields divisible by twelve. The math should be simple this way. If a recipe yields thirty-six cookies and you've asked swappers to provide six dozen, everyone will need to make two batches.

Notice that I don't instruct you to "double" the recipe. Your stand mixer, unless it is the largest, professional-size KitchenAid, won't be able to accommodate a doubled quantity of most of these cookie doughs. So you'll

have to mix two batches separately (there's usually no need to wash out the mixing bowl between batches) in order to end up with twice as many cookies.

When you want everyone to bake up an additional dozen or so for snacking, I recommend mixing a full extra recipe, rather than cutting a recipe in half (which can be tricky and yield not-so-hot results). When you make extra dough, either freeze what you don't bake (best for most of the cookies in this book) or bake it all and freeze the excess (best for bars). You'll find more information on freezing in each recipe.

"A good, simple, homemade cookie is preferable to all the storebought cookies one can find."

JAMES BEARD

people you invite, the more cookies everyone will have to bake. The math says otherwise. When you've arrived at the number of cookies you'd like each guest to take home, you've also determined the number of cookies each person must bake. That's it: Everyone goes home with the same number of cookies that they came with.

To divide the cookies among swappers, follow this basic equation:

$$\frac{\text{\# of cookies}}{\text{\# of people}} = \frac{\text{\# of each cookie}}{\text{type per person}}$$

To illustrate, let's say you've got eight people (include yourself here) who have baked forty-eight cookies each. Forty-eight divided by eight equals six. So you'll direct the swappers to take six of each type of cookie, which means they'll have an assortment of forty-eight cookies at swap's end. If your equation has a remainder, simply make sure that everyone takes an extra cookie or two of their choice.

One more thing: If your idea of "cookie swap" is "cookie *eat* and swap," you'll need to make some minor adjustments. There are two basic options. If your guests are light nibblers, there's no need to bake extras; people can just eat more cookies at the party and swap fewer later. In the case of the party of eight above, you might have each person set aside eight cookies on an "eat now" table, and then take home five of each (instead of six) at the end. However, if you're a believer in more is more, ask everyone to bake an extra dozen (see Gimme More, opposite). Any extras from the "eat now" pile can always be divided up later—or kept as spoils of the swap by the chef in chief.

YOU'RE INVITED . . .

Now that you've stashed away your abacus, it's time to get creative and put together the invitations. You'll want to cover all the basics, of course, and give a hint of the fun that's to come. Let your guests know whether the swap is a special midmorning coffee break, a wine-and-cheese tasting on book club night, or a Galleta Fiesta (that's sort of Spanish for "cookie party") on Cinco de Mayo. And if you're serving more than sweets, be sure to spell that out, too. People want to know whether they should arrive fully fed or leave room for margaritas and your famous guacamole.

So many cookies— in so little time!

It's possible to adapt a store-bought party invitation for the purpose, but most of these won't have enough room for all of the delicious details. Besides, homemade invites are more fun to make and to receive. If you're crafty, you could scrapbook an invitation or hand-letter it on interesting paper; or jump on to the computer and design an invitation using The Print Shop or other software. Online photo services such as Shutterfly.com offer reasonably priced custom photo invitations as well.

Here's what to include:

* **What:** Some of your invitees may not know what a cookie swap is. Give them the lowdown. This is also the place to mention your April in Paris or Winter Wonderland theme.
* **Why:** As if you need a reason! But if there is one, state it here.
* **When:** This is easy—it's the date and time.
* **Where:** Provide the address. If people are traveling from hither and yon, enclose directions and/or a little map (or promise to e-mail them later on).
* **How:** This is where you lay out how many cookies to bake, how to pack them, and what else, if anything, guests will need to bring to the swap. Ask everyone to tell you what they plan to bring when they RSVP (you can ask them for the recipe, too).

If you don't have lots of serving pieces (don't worry, you're not alone), or if you're throwing a themed fete, feel free to ask people to bring along a platter or festive decoration. You can even request a different item—Max's silver punch bowl, Martha's miniature maracas—from each person.

***

Now simply drop your invites in the mail, hand deliver them, or e-mail them. (E-mail may not be Miss Manners' choice, but it does save time, money, and trees. E-mail also makes it easy for your invitees to RSVP, ask questions, and send recipes if you've requested them. So if this is the right step for you, politely tell Miss Manners to button up.)

COMPANY IS COMING

You've chosen a date, you've chosen a theme, you even know what you want to bake . . . now what? It's time to get organized. The handy time line that follows will lay out what to do and when, so your prep and party will go smoothly—and you'll actually get to enjoy it. You can use the helpful checklist on page 11 to make sure all your ducks are in a row.

"The ornament of a house is the friends who frequent it."
RALPH WALDO EMERSON

SAMPLE SWAP INVITATION

Every swap invitation, no matter how elaborate or bare bones, should include the six Ws—who, what, where, when, why, how—plus an R (for RSVP).

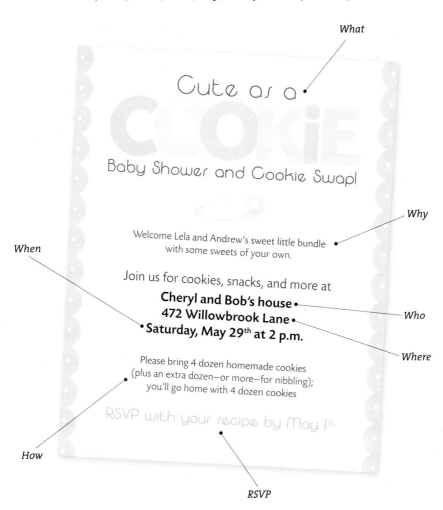

What

Why

When

Who

Where

How

RSVP

Cute as a

COOKIE

Baby Shower and Cookie Swap!

Welcome Lela and Andrew's sweet little bundle
with some sweets of your own.

Join us for cookies, snacks, and more at
Cheryl and Bob's house
472 Willowbrook Lane
Saturday, May 29th at 2 p.m.

Please bring 4 dozen homemade cookies
(plus an extra dozen—or more—for nibbling);
you'll go home with 4 dozen cookies

RSVP with your recipe by May 1st

*Cheater's Petits Fours,
p. 198*

Two to Four Weeks Ahead

* Send your invitations. As responses come in, keep a list of what everyone will be bringing to make sure you don't have a cookie overlap (other than a sandwich cookie, of course). Get in touch with any stragglers so you can firm up your numbers.
* Mail order any items that you can't get locally: ingredients, equipment, cookie tins, gift bags, party favors, decorations, and so on. (For help locating particular items, see Resources, page 216.)

One Week Ahead

* Check in with your guests, confirm their cookie choices, and remind them how many cookies they're supposed to bring. If you want to swap recipes along with cookies, ask guests to provide them.
* If you're serving snacks, plan your menu. Shop for cookie ingredients and nonperishable items, including equipment, decorations, party favors, bottled water, soda, wine, and beer.
* No party's complete without tunes: Put together a special playlist (this is especially key if your party has a theme).
* Mix and freeze cookie dough, if your recipe allows for this.

* Buy some tented cards for identifying each type of cookie, or make your own.

Three Days Ahead

* Do the rest of your shopping (don't forget to buy milk!).
* Wrap any party favors and prizes.
* Straighten up the house or, if swapping off-site, drop off any folding tables, takeaway containers, or decorations that you'll need.

One Day Ahead

* Bake your cookies and, once cool, store them in airtight containers so they stay fresh for tomorrow. Make copies of your own recipes if you wish.
* Set up the swap spot. Choose an area that's a bit separate from where your guests will be chatting and carousing, and put a table there. Plan to have snacks and drinks in one place, and then to move to the area around the table for the swap. Not only does this add some drama to the event, but it removes any temptation to sneak a taste of the cookies before the swap (trust me— sticky fingers abound when sweets sit in plain view). Spread a cloth over the table and put up your decorations. Arrange enough platters, trays, and baskets to accommodate all of the

COOKIE SWAP CHECKLIST

This checklist will keep your party prep on track. You may want to photocopy it each time you have a swap.

At Least Two Weeks Ahead
- Select your theme, if any
- Determine a venue; reserve if necessary.
- Compile a guest list.
- Make and send invitations.
- Figure out what necessities are available locally and what, if anything, needs to be bought online. Order online stuff.

One Week Ahead
- Confirm your guests' cookie selections (and make sure there aren't any duplicates).
- Plan your drinks/food menu.
- Compile a music playlist.
- Do your local shopping for any decorations, prizes, favors, nonperishable ingredients, etc., you didn't buy online.

- Make and freeze your cookie dough/cookies, if possible (see individual recipes for instructions).

Three Days Ahead
- Shop for perishable ingredients and last-minute items.
- Do the clean sweep: Eradicate dust bunnies.
- Bundle your favors and prizes.

The Day Before
- Bake your cookies.
- Prep your party food.
- Decorate your space.

Swap Day
- Concoct beverages, finish and plate party food.
- Put on some music, and let the games begin!

cookies; if people are toting their own serving pieces, leave room for those.

* Write out the tented cookie ID cards (or set out some pens so guests can do this when they arrive).

* Do any beverage and food prep that you can: Squeeze lemon juice for lemonade, cut vegetables for crudités, make dips and spreads, and so on.

It's Swap Day!

* Arrange the pre-swap food area with disposable cups, napkins, and any plates and utensils you'll be

KICKIN' IT OLD SCHOOL :: THE TRADITIONAL CHRISTMAS SWAP

For many of us, when we think cookie swap, we also think Christmas. This makes perfectly good sense—the cookie exchange originated as a holiday celebration with a purpose, one that allowed people to trade cookies (and chit chat) rather than spend days chained to their ovens. And while cookie swaps have expanded to include all sorts of occasions, the popularity of holiday exchanges hasn't waned. In fact, the legendary Wellesley Cookie Exchange (so legendary that it is capitalized), which was started by a now-retired nurse named Mary Bevilacqua, is still going strong after almost forty years.

As with all the best timeworn traditions, you can celebrate the old while adding touches of the new. Here's how to throw a classic Christmas cookie swap with a contemporary twist:

Get the word out. Every year people seem to get busier around the holidays. Spread the word around Thanksgiving, and send out your invitations several weeks in advance to ensure that you'll get a good crowd.

Get sentimental. Throw a log on the fire, tack up the mistletoe, and put Bing's "White Christmas" on the playlist. This is the time of year to make your grandmother's pfeffernusse or the gingerbread men you loved so much when you were little. Ask your co-swappers to bake and bring their favorite cookies and share stories about why they are special.

Get crafty. Set up a separate table and chairs for ornament making. Provide ornament hooks and inexpensive metal ball ornaments, mini pom-poms, paint, glue, glitter, googly eyes, pipe cleaners—whatever strikes your fancy—and let your guests go at it. While their ornaments dry, people can gather 'round for carols or sip bevvies from Christmas stocking drink holders (available at Oriental Trading; see Resources, page 216).

Get into the spirit. Ask everyone to bring a new toy for a local toy drive program. Go to Secretsanta.org to find one in your area. Or sponsor a coat drive: Have folks contribute a gently used coat, which you'll donate after the party (for information on where to drop coats in your area, visit www.onewarmcoat.org).

using. Or consider going green: use cute, mismatched tag-sale teacups and china instead. Real dishware makes cleanup a bit more labor intensive, but it has a lot more character than plastic and paper, and won't jam up a landfill later.

* Once you've laid out your table, whip up any noshes that haven't already been prepared.

* Onc hour before the swap, put on your music, arrange your own cookies on one of the platters, set up your bar, and set out your eats. Oh, and relax—it's party time!

SWAPPING MADE SIMPLE

As your swappers arrive, make room on the table for each person's cookies, and transfer any intended extras to another platter near the rest of the food. Once all the cookies are displayed, you can snap some pics of the whole spread; these make sweet mementos when sent out along with your thank-you notes. And if you haven't set aside any cookies for snacking, keep an eye on your swap table—even when cheese platters, chili, *and* shrimp cocktail are being offered, the lure of those cookies can be mighty powerful.

After everyone's had a chance to mix and mingle and have a nibble or two, it's time to get down to business. Gather your guests around the table, making sure each person has a takeaway container in hand. If people want to share stories about their cookies or describe what they made, now is the time. Then, before letting the mob loose, lay down the laws of the swap:

1. Everyone should move around the table in one direction.
2. At each plate, each person should take X number of cookies (and a recipe card, if there is one) and move on.
3. No "storing" cookies in your mouth or pockets!

And that's it—you've swapped successfully. When it's time to say good-bye, hand out warm thanks and compliments along with your party favors.

THANKS FOR THE MEMORIES

A cookie swap is an occasion for sharing cookies, of course, but it's also a chance to share the recipes for new favorites. If you are hosting, think

". . . Pastry is like feathers—it is like snow. It is in fact good for you, a digestive!"

M. F. K. FISHER

CONTAIN YOURSELF :: SERVING PIECES AND TOTES

Sure, your friends can schlep their baked goods in all manner of Tupperware and tin—but they'll need something to display them on once they get to the party, and another something in which to take them away. To keep it simple, you could ask your guests to bring two containers: one for displaying and swapping, and a second for collecting the cookies they will take home. If you want to get a little fancier, try designing a charmingly eclectic display table using your own trays, platters, baskets, and/or cake stands. Pull together mismatched pieces in similar materials, tones, or color families (all glass, for example, or bright hues) and unify everything with a tablecloth and clusters of low candles or small bunches of flowers. Or invest in new serving trays just for the party. There are plenty of inexpensive choices at chain stores like Target, IKEA, and Pier 1 Imports as well as online (see Resources, page 216)—I'm betting you'll get your money's worth. And after the success of your first cookie swap, you'll end up using them again and again.

Whatever you decide, do your best to arrange these containers ahead of time. As the cookies come in you can decide which ones look best where. Then when swap time comes, you can provide gift bags, cookie tins, Chinese takeout containers, or cardboard bakery boxes as totes, or just let guests retrieve their original containers for easy gather-and-go.

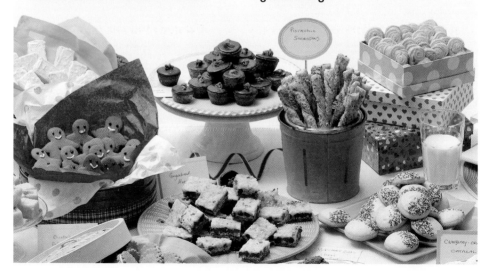

about the following ways to collect and distribute the recipes from the party, to give your guests a lasting memory of the event:

Get Carded: Ask guests to write up enough recipe cards to distribute to every guest at the party. They can keep these ultra-simple, writing on traditional blue-lined index cards, or they can gct a bit more intricate with designed recipe cards (available at www.personalrecipecards.com or www.finestationery.com; custom cards can be created at www.smilebox .com/recipe-cards/). When setting the table for the swap, leave space for the recipes next to each basket or platter of cookies. Swappers can pick up the recipes as they pick up cookies. Provide everyone with a decorated envelope to hold the individual cards.

For the Neatnik: If organization is your middle name, ask your guests to e-mail a recipe a few days in advance, which you can print out and distribute at the swap. And if persistence is your *other* middle name, you might manage to shake the recipes out of people when they RSVP, giving you time to print them out (get as elaborate with your desktop publishing as you like)

and collate them into embellished boxes. You can hand these out as favors at the end of the party.

Book 'Em: Ask everyone to e-mail their recipe shortly after the swap. In the days following the party, compile the recipes into an e-cookbook (for more on this, see "Reality Bytes," page 130), and send a copy to each guest, to print out or keep on the computer for future reference.

"Dig" It: Remember those digital pics you took of everyone's cookies before the swap? Now's the time to use them: Put together an album of the party, complete with recipes, using an online photo service, such as kodakgallery .com, shutterfly.com, or snapfish.com. Send a copy to everyone who attended (some of these services will mail directly to a list of recipients, so you can avoid going to the post office).

Yet Another Reason to Join Facebook: As I write this, 400 million people have joined this online social networking site. By the time this book

Blank recipe cards make for sweet party favors—and may inspire your friends to throw a swap of their own.

EVERYTHING JUST SO :: THE CONTROL FREAK'S COOKIE SWAP

Say you are the kind of person who likes to control every detail of a party, down to the color of the last cocktail napkin (some might say I'm describing *myself* here). You worry that you won't like the way Aunt Sally's oversize snickerdoodles will look next to your best friend Trixie's misshapen granola bars. And what if Trixie's husband decides to do the baking and makes those oat bran hockey pucks again?! Try to relax, and remind yourself that cookie swapping is not about perfection, it's about appreciating everyone's efforts.

However, if you know that no amount of deep breathing will soothe your nerves, or if you have a particular flavor theme—Chocomania! Cuckoo for Coconut!—you want everyone to follow, you can suggest or assign specific recipes in each invitation. But err on the side of caution here: This is best attempted only if your guests are good-humored people who understand your perfection "problem" and don't mind bending to your will. (Some people might, in fact, be grateful that you've relieved them of the burden of choosing.) It will help, in any case, if you are gracious in your bossiness; you might include a small token of your appreciation along with your invite and the recipe you've chosen, perhaps a new set of measuring spoons, a colorful rubber spatula, or—dare I say it—a copy of this book!

comes out, chances are good that millions more will be members. If everyone on your guest list is on, you can create a group just for your cookie swap, invite your guests to join, and use the group page to post photos and recipes from the party. A Facebook group page is also a convenient place to post information and answer questions pre-swap.

Chapter 2

SWAPPER'S DELIGHT

THE COOKIE BAKER'S BAG OF TRICKS

Every great baker has a set of preferred ingredients, equipment, and tricks that he keeps tucked in his mental back pocket. I've been baking for years, both at home and on the job, so I've had a long time (and my fair share of "Oops!" moments) to test and refine my list. Here's what I use to turn out delicious cookies time and again; whether you're a professional pastry chef or a wide-eyed newbie, I hope you'll find these tips helpful, too.

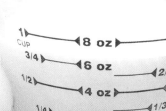

Lighten Up
TESTING YOUR LEAVENING

Can't remember when you first opened that can of baking powder or box of baking soda? If you have any doubt about the freshness of either, there are easy ways to test their power to poof. To test baking powder, mix a teaspoon with ½ cup of water. If the baking powder bubbles vigorously, it still works. For baking soda, mix ½ teaspoon with two teaspoons of vinegar. You probably remember this combo from grade school science, and you want the same results now as then: If the mixture bubbles up, you're good to go.

COOKIE SWAPPER'S PANTRY

By and large, the cookies in this book are made with ingredients available in any supermarket. There are very few specialty items (like coarse sanding sugar and crystallized ginger) that might require a tiny bit of legwork, but if your pantry, refrigerator, and freezer are stocked with most of the items listed below, you won't have much last-minute shopping.

Baking Powder: This leavening agent will give a lift to your cookies and bars. Before you buy a new can of the stuff, check the expiration date to make sure it will still work when you get it home. Once you open it, store it in a cool, dry place; it should be good for six months. Keep in mind that baking powder loses its ability to raise baked goods when it comes in contact with moisture. Always be sure to measure it with a dry spoon, and don't keep it uncovered in a humid kitchen.

Baking Soda: Many cookie recipes call for baking soda in place of or in addition to baking powder. Baking soda will keep for many months if stored in an airtight container at room temperature. Exposed in an open container, however, it will absorb moisture from the air (as well as all sorts of odors, which is why you keep it in your fridge, after all), and won't be suitable for baking after a few weeks. So when you buy a new box for baking, transfer it to an airtight container for safekeeping.

Butter: The salt content in salted butter can vary considerably from brand to brand, so for the sake of consistency I only use unsalted butter and then add salt to a recipe as necessary. Butter has gotten quite expensive in the past few years, so I stock up on it when I'm shopping at my local warehouse club. It will keep in the refrigerator for several weeks, and in the freezer for several months.

For baking purposes, it's always best to buy sticks—which are easy to measure and cut—instead of tubs. And before you add butter to any dough, pay special attention to whether the recipe calls for it chilled, at room temperature, or melted; this handling makes

THE BENTLEY OF BITTERSWEET :: PREMIUM CHOCOLATE CHIPS

When making chocolate chip cookie dough, some bakers like to substitute chopped bittersweet chocolate bars for chocolate chips because of premium chocolate's superior flavor. But I love the teardrop shape of chocolate chips and I love how they hold this shape during baking (unlike chocolate bars, chips contain stabilizers that prevent them from fully melting in the oven).

Supermarket brands are just fine, but nothing vaults a chocolate chip cookie into the pantheon of great baked goods like a bag of Ghirardelli 60% Cacao Bittersweet Chocolate Chips or Schokinag Bittersweet Chocolate Chips (see Resources, page 216). Try baking a batch of cookies with these expensive—but worth it—chips and see if you agree.

a big difference in the texture of the final product.

A word about margarine and shortening: In my opinion, butter makes *much* more delicious cookies than margarine or solid shortening, which is why I use it almost exclusively in these recipes. I know that bright yellow tub of pretend butter can be tempting when you really want cookies and don't have the real stuff on hand, but I'm here to warn you—you won't be happy with the results!

Chocolate: When brownie and chocolate cookie recipes call for unsweetened baking chocolate, inexpensive squares work just as well as premium brands. But if a recipe calls for semisweet or bittersweet chocolate, spend the extra money on best-quality bars from a chocolate maker like Lindt or Ghirardelli. It will make a difference.

Chocolate chips are practically a food group in my house. I always have bags of semisweet, white, and mini morsels around to satisfy spur-of-the-moment baking urges.

Keep a box of unsweetened cocoa powder on hand to make chocolate shortbread cookies and chocolate-flavored royal icing. Natural and Dutch-process cocoa powders are both suitable for cookie baking (I generally bake with Dutch-process because I prefer its mellow flavor, but this is a

A COCOA CODA :: CHOCOLATE FOR EVERY PURPOSE

So many chocolates, so little time . . . If you find yourself in the enviable position of having to choose among chocolate types, it helps to know the differences between them.

Unsweetened chocolate is made from processed cacao beans, and consists entirely of cocoa solids and cocoa butter that have been extracted from the beans. It contains no sugar—hence, its name and straight-up, unadulterated flavor. Unsweetened chocolate works well in brownie recipes, where you are already adding fat in the form of butter and you want strong chocolate flavor.

Bittersweet, semisweet, and milk chocolates are made by mixing unsweetened chocolate with sugar and, in the case of milk chocolate, powdered or condensed milk. All three are great in cookies, melted, or as chips or chunks.

In contrast, white chocolate is made with cocoa butter, milk solids, and sugar. Since it contains no cocoa solids, it isn't technically chocolate at all. Any chocolate flavor it gets comes from cocoa butter, so when buying white chocolate look for a brand that contains at least 20 percent cocoa butter; it will have the best flavor.

Carob is a chocolate substitute made from the roasted and ground pods of the carob tree, a Mediterranean evergreen. Naturally sweeter than unsweetened chocolate (which, if you've ever tasted any, you know is quite bitter and not sweet at all!), in some Mediterranean regions it was traditionally used as a sweetener (in some places it still is). Because carob is naturally sweet, baking chips made with it require less sugar or other sweetener to make them palatable. Carob has a distinctive flavor that's not entirely chocolatelike. For some, it can be an acquired taste.

Use a combo of dark and milk chocolates to jazz up standard chocolate chippers.

personal choice). When substituting one for the other, be aware that Dutch cocoa has been treated with an alkali to neutralize its acids, while natural cocoa powder is still acidic. This is important if you are using a leavening agent, such as baking powder or baking soda, in your recipe. Recipes using Dutch cocoa employ baking powder, while recipes with natural cocoa employ baking soda, which reacts with those acids. If you plan on swapping one type of cocoa powder for the other, you'll have to swap leavenings, too.

Cookies and crackers: If you are pressed for time or want to keep your kitchen cool, boxes of vanilla wafers, graham crackers, saltines, and shortbread cookies will give you a head start in preparing for a cookie swap. For recipes using these ingredients, see Chapter 12.

Cornmeal: I love the crunch and color of yellow cornmeal and try to sneak it into cookie recipes whenever I can. (I never use white, since it doesn't crisp and brighten my cookies the same way.) Try to buy stone-ground cornmeal from a small or organic mill, such as Bob's Red Mill or Hodgson Mills; these cornmeals have better flavor and are more nutritious to boot. Stone-ground cornmeal is available at most supermarkets and natural foods stores and adds a wonderfully wholesome flavor and texture to many baked goods.

(If you'd like to experiment with adding cornmeal to one of your favorite recipes, simply substitute an equal amount of cornmeal for no more than one-third of the flour. Since the protein in flour gives cookies their structure, substituting more cornmeal than this might compromise the structure of the cookies and make them too crumbly to hold together after baking.)

Eggs: For consistent results, always use large eggs. White or brown, it's your call.

Flour: Most of the recipes in this book were tested with unbleached all-purpose flour (I like the King Arthur brand). In general, unbleached all-purpose flour has just the right amount of protein for cookies, making them pleasantly chewy, with good structure. Cookies made with softer cake flour tend to fall apart, while cookies baked with bread flour can be tough like breadsticks.

For cookies, unbleached all-purpose flour is usually best.

Food Coloring: In a pinch, a four-color supermarket set of liquid food coloring will do. However, if you can get your hands on a larger set of gel colors (they come in eight- and twelve-packs; see Resources, page 216), you will be able to get much more creative when icing your cookies.

Use either type of food coloring sparingly. Pastel-colored cookies are almost always more aesthetically pleasing than neon-bright ones. If you're using liquid food coloring, begin by adding just a drop to your icing, stirring it in to gauge the intensity of the color. For gel coloring, dip the end of a toothpick or wooden skewer into the color and then into the icing and stir to see how much color you get.

Jam and Jelly: I use jam and jelly all the time to fill thumbprints, pinwheels, rugelach, and Linzer cookies. Different recipes call for different types of jam. Feel free to substitute favorite flavors for the ones suggested. Seeded or seedless is a matter of personal preference, too. (For tips on seeding jam, see page 44.)

Meringue Powder: Traditionally, whipped raw egg whites were used to give royal icing stability and a nice, smooth texture. Nowadays we don't like to use raw egg in icing, especially when it might be consumed by children, pregnant women, or anyone with a compromised immune system. So we substitute meringue powder, which is a combination of dried egg whites, sugar, and gum stabilizers that gives royal icing a beautiful sheen and fluffy texture. One jar will last for months or years. See Resources, page 216, if you can't find this essential cookie decorator's item at your local specialty foods store.

Molasses: An essential ingredient in gingerbread and spice cookies. Look for dark molasses, not light (which is too mild) or blackstrap (which is too bitter).

Nutella: If you can resist eating it right from the jar, keep some of this delicious imported chocolate-hazelnut spread in the pantry to fill thumbprint and sandwich cookies.

Nuts: I store at least six kinds of nuts (almonds, walnuts, pecans, pine nuts, hazelnuts, pistachios) in ziplock bags in my freezer (they go rancid quickly if stored at room temperature). Frozen, they'll keep for up to year.

Oats: Buy old-fashioned (rolled) oats for oatmeal cookies. Avoid "quick-cooking" oats, which have been chopped up into little pieces and won't give your cookies the chewy texture that you want. Also avoid "instant" oats, which have been precooked and dehydrated and won't give your cookies any texture at all.

Peanut Butter: Avoid freshly ground peanut butter from the natural foods store when making cookies. It is too grainy and coarse for baking. Supermarket brands such as Jif, Skippy, and Peter Pan have the smooth texture necessary for making the least greasy, most tender peanut butter cookies. If you prefer peanut butter with less added sugar, choose a commercial brand like Smucker's, which is additive-free but still has a smooth texture.

Spices: Ground cinnamon is a must, because it is used in so many types of cookies. Ground ginger is also an important cookie-baking spice. Nutmeg, allspice, and ground cloves are nice to have, too. Buy anise and fennel seeds when you need them. Grind black pepper fresh from your pepper mill to use in savory cookie recipes.

Sprinkles: I buy large containers of sprinkles at my warehouse club when I see them, so I don't run out (they seem to disappear quickly whenever there's ice cream around!). I also like to order multicolored nonpareils (see Resources, page 216) for a change of pace.

Sugar: I have an entire pantry shelf devoted to the different types of sugar I use, in descending order of importance: granulated white sugar, light brown sugar, dark brown sugar, confectioners' sugar, white and colored sanding sugars, and turbinado sugar (or Sugar in the Raw). I occasionally use other types of sweeteners, including honey, maple syrup, and corn syrup, which will keep in the pantry for months.

I'm a traditionalist when it comes to cookies, so I haven't baked much with alternative and artificial sweeteners such as agave nectar, stevia, Splenda, and NutraSweet. I can't offer much advice about using them in place of sugar, but I urge you to take care and follow package recommendations—not all of these are appropriate for baking, and substituting isn't always a matter of replacing sugar with an equal amount of the alternative.

Vanilla Extract: I use only pure vanilla extract, which I buy in big bottles at my local warehouse club. Artificial vanilla is a lot cheaper, but tastes terrible in my opinion.

Sugar gets its color from molasses. The darker the sugar, the higher its molasses content and flavor.

You can cut dough in a variety of shapes as long as the cutters are about equal in size.

EQUIPMENT ESSENTIALS

Cookie baking doesn't require many tools; a mixer, a spatula, a few baking sheets and pans, a rolling pin, and some cookie cutters will do you. But because I bake all the time, my arsenal is a bit more extensive. Here are the items I use often.

Baking Pan: The bar cookies in this book are baked in a 9-by-13-inch metal baking pan. You can substitute a glass baking dish of the same size, but your bars will bake a little faster, so check them 10 minutes before the suggested baking time is up, and keep a close watch thereafter so they don't overbake. You can substitute two 8-by-8-inch metal baking pans if you don't have the larger size, but again, batter baked in smaller pans will cook more quickly; watch your bars carefully and pull them from the oven when they're done, so they don't dry out.

Baking Sheets: Heavy-duty stainless steel baking sheets brown cookies without scorching them, and won't warp even after years of use. Rimless baking sheets are great for sliding cookies, still on parchment paper, right onto wire cooling racks. When I decorate cookies with sprinkles, edible glitter, or drizzled chocolate I do so on a wire rack set on top of a rimmed baking sheet to contain the mess. Most home ovens won't accommodate anything larger than a half-sheet pan size, which measures 18 by 13 inches.

Cookie Cutters: Expensive copper cookie cutters are a luxury (which I indulge in too often—see Resources, page 216), but metal of any kind is preferable to plastic, which won't cut as cleanly.

Cookie Scoop: I use a cookie scoop, which resembles a small spring-loaded ice cream scoop, to get perfectly rounded, perfectly uniform balls of drop cookie dough (see The Scoop on Scoops, opposite). If you don't have cookie scoops, measure out your dough the old-fashioned way, using a heaping tablespoon or teaspoon. Don't fret if your cookies don't come out perfectly shaped—that never bothered Grandma! The cookies will taste just as good.

Double Boiler: A two-pot contraption that's essential for melting chocolate

THE SCOOP ON SCOOPS

There are several good reasons to make each cookie the same size and shape as the previous one. Size affects baking time. You want each cookie in the batch to be the same size so that they'll all be done at the same time. If your cookies vary from each other by even a teaspoon or so, you'll very likely have to overbake the smaller ones to give the larger ones enough time to bake through. For swapping, it's nice to offer uniformly sized and shaped cookies, so that everyone gets equally beautiful examples to take home. And if you portion out your dough evenly and accurately, you are more likely to wind up with the number of cookies you expected than if you just eyeball it every time.

A cookie scoop will help you to evenly measure out drop cookie dough as well as dough for many types of cookies shaped by hand. The scoop's spring action guarantees a clean release, which means an almost perfectly shaped cookie. (A melon baller won't work as well, since there's no neat way to release the dough.) These scoops are available at baking supply stores (see Resources, page 216) and come in sizes to approximate heaping teaspoons (which measure about 1¾ teaspoons) and heaping tablespoons (about 1⅓ tablespoons), as well as a larger size to make jumbo cookies and to scoop muffin batter. I most often use my "tablespoon" cookie scoop, but I own them all so I can make uniformly tiny, medium, and extra-large cookies.

without burning it (it's also useful for heating milk). If you don't have a double boiler, you can improvise one by setting a metal bowl over a pan of simmering water. To do this, put two inches of water in a medium-size saucepan and bring it to a bare simmer. Set a stainless steel bowl over the water, making sure the bowl is big enough to rest on the edge of the pan but not so deep that it touches the water.

Electric Mixer: A heavy-duty stand mixer from KitchenAid is expensive but wonderful to have. If you are buying a handheld mixer instead, look for a model with thin metal beaters, which can handle thick cookie dough better than old-fashioned beaters with metal shafts down the center.

Food Processor: I use my food processor for chopping large quantities of nuts, as well as for mixing sticky doughs like the cream cheese dough I use to make rugelach (see page 77).

Measuring Cups and Spoons: Accurate measuring is the cornerstone of successful baking. Use "dry" plastic or metal measuring cups for dry ingredients, and use the "dip-and-sweep" method: Scoop up ingredients with the measuring cup and level them off with the edge of a knife, scraping any excess back into the canister. Small amounts of dry ingredients should be measured with measuring spoons. For liquids, use clear glass measuring cups with pour spouts. Look at the incremental measurement lines on the side of the cup at eye level to be sure that you have filled it to just the right line.

Mixing Bowls: An inexpensive set of nesting glass mixing bowls will

come in handy for premeasuring and organizing ingredients. It is great to also have a few stainless steel bowls for mixing doughs and improvising a double boiler (see page 24).

Parchment Paper: Save yourself the heartbreak of sticking cookies and the hassle of scrubbing cookie sheets by lining your pans with parchment paper before baking any kind of cookie. See "Stuck on You," opposite.

Pastry Bag and Tips: I like disposable plastic pastry bags (see Resources, page 216), because I hate to wash reusable pastry bags, and often need several bags when I am using several colors of icing. Since I use a pastry bag only a few times a year, I allow myself this un-green habit. If you wouldn't be able to live with yourself, use a reusable polyester bag, turning it inside out after use and washing it immediately with hot, soapy water. Stand it, still inside out, over a tall water glass or empty long-neck bottle, to dry completely (otherwise mold and mildew may grow on it) before storing it away for future use.

Although I have a deluxe, professional set of tips, I usually use only the very smallest plain tips to decorate cookies (they're great for stripes, squiggles, and dots).

Rolling Pin: Choose the style you are most comfortable with: I use a French-style pin, which is a hardwood cylinder without handles, since this is what I learned on in cooking school. But an American rolling pin with handles or a tapered rolling pin, with slim ends, will also work just fine.

Spatulas: Three types of spatula come in handy for cookie baking. Use a rubber spatula to scrape down the sides of your mixing bowl when

STUCK ON YOU   A PARCHMENT PAPER LOVE SONG

I am on a crusade to convince anyone who bakes even occasionally to order a hundred-count box of precut parchment paper from the Baker's Catalogue (see Resources, page 216). If you've never used this wonder-paper before, you might think you do just fine without it. But believe me, once you start baking cookies on it, you will never go back.

Parchment paper, which has been impregnated with silicone, is perfectly nonstick. Even the stickiest cookies will slide right off of the paper once they have cooled. Many cookie recipes call for ungreased baking sheets, since cookies baked on greased sheets tend to spread too much. Feel free to use parchment in these if you wish—it will prevent spreading, and make cleanup easier.

Baking on parchment saves time and makes baking easier. If you portion out your dough onto paper, you won't have to cool your cookie sheets between batches. When one batch is ready to come out of the oven, simply slide the cookies, still on the paper, onto a wire rack and slide the next batch onto the baking sheet and return it to the oven. Reuse paper from earlier batches to cut down on waste. Using parchment will save you from scrubbing your cookie sheets when you're done. No cleanup—just toss the paper and that's it.

If you keep an ample stash of parchment paper, I guarantee it will come in handy for many tasks besides lining cookie sheets: Roll out sticky pie and cookie dough between two sheets of parchment, place pizza or bread on parchment and slide it onto a baking stone without sticking, create a parchment collar for a soufflé dish, fold parchment into a cornet to pipe chocolate decorations onto cookies and cakes, wrap it into little packets for steaming vegetables and fish, and on and on . . .

making dough. Use a wide, thin metal or nylon spatula to remove cookies from a cookie sheet. And use a small metal offset spatula (which is like a long, dull butter knife with a bend in it) to spread icing or chocolate onto cooled cookies.

Storage Containers: My mother, the owner of one of the world's great Tupperware collections, would be proud of my set of well-organized airtight plastic containers, in every shape and size, which takes up a large cabinet in my kitchen. I use them to store baked and cooled cookies. I also use them to transport cookies to swap locations, unless I've been directed to pack the cookies in a tin or wrap them on a platter instead.

Whisk: A whisk always comes in handy: to make sure that melted chocolate is smooth, to break up whole eggs, to whip up small batches of Royal Icing (page 139), to mix together dry ingredients before adding them to the wet ingredients, and so much more.

"My therapist told me the way to achieve true inner peace is to finish what I start. So far today, I have finished two bags of M&M's and a chocolate cake. I feel better already."

DAVE BARRY

Wire Racks: Transfer hot cookies to wire racks to cool. You should have at least a couple of these, to accommodate all of the cookies you will be baking for your swap.

FRESH IS BEST

Guess who wants to eat stale cookies. Nobody! When you sign up for a swap, you should contribute the freshest cookies you can. The other guests may want to hold on to them for a day or two, so they shouldn't be halfway to tough and dry before the party even starts.

But this doesn't mean you have to make three dozen cookies from scratch two hours before the swap. With some planning and preparation, you can easily provide freshly baked cookies with a minimum of last-minute work.

* **Choose a Keeper:** If you want to be done with your baking ahead of time, bake cookies that will stay fresh for many (rather than just a few) days. Biscotti, meringues, and no-bake treats that begin with store-bought cookies all fare well. (Conversely, sandwich cookies with moist or buttery fillings are best eaten sooner rather than later, although you can bake the cookies ahead of time and fill them just before the swap.) Try any of these long-lasting options: Classic Almond Biscotti (two to three weeks), page 149; Raspberry Meringue Kisses (one week), page 163; and Saltine Toffee Bark (one week), page 196.

* **Use Your Freezer:** Many types of cookie dough freeze well, and I've given specific directions for freezing wherever relevant (these recipes are marked with a Freeze Me! icon). Drop cookies can be formed into balls, frozen, and placed directly from the freezer into the oven (you may need to increase the bake time slightly). Making the cookie dough ahead of time, it is possible to bake four dozen cookies in less than an hour. Icebox cookie dough can be shaped into logs, wrapped in a double layer of plastic and then a layer of heavy-duty aluminum foil, and frozen for weeks; defrost it overnight in the refrigerator before baking. Slicing and baking four dozen icebox cookies will take less than an hour as well.

Blondies and brownies, once baked and cooled, can be wrapped in a double layer of plastic and a layer of heavy-duty aluminum foil, and then frozen for up to one month. Defrost them overnight in the refrigerator or for several hours on the countertop. Partially defrosted, they're easy to slice into neat pieces. Allow them to defrost fully before packing them up for the swap.

* **Pack It Up:** Cookies turn stale more quickly when exposed to air and moisture. Once your cookies are cooled, pack them snugly in airtight containers or ziplock bags to keep them fresh. Store like cookies together—crispy with crispy and soft with soft; packing moist cookies with crackly cookies will make the crackly cookies take on moisture and lose crunch, and vice versa. If your cookies are sticky or delicate, pack them in layers, between sheets of parchment paper.

Don't refrigerate the cookies—at cold temperatures above freezing baked goods tend to dry out more quickly than they will at room temperature.

Different types of cookies may require different kinds of handling at every stage to preserve freshness, so look for specific tips in the introduction to each chapter and in individual recipes.

Plastic or glass containers with tight-fitting plastic lids are ideal for cookie storage (and keep the cookies fresher than tins do).

Chapter 3

DROP EVERYTHING!

DELECTABLE DROP COOKIES

There's a reason back-of-the-bag chocolate chip cookies and top-of-the-box oatmeal raisins are the go-to recipes for kids first learning how to bake. Ingredient lists are short. There's no rolling or shaping, and no painstaking decorating. And you can pretty much bend the recipes to your will, tweaking the add-ins (substituting milk chocolate chunks for bittersweet chips, say, or Craisins for raisins) as you please. As long as you don't mess with the makeup of the dough itself, you're pretty much guaranteed success. Yup—making drop cookies is child's play.

These cookies offer convenience, too. The dough can be mixed when you have the time, and then frozen for up to a month and baked off when needed. Just scoop equal-size balls of unbaked cookie dough onto a parchment-lined baking sheet, freeze until firm (no more than 1 hour), transfer the frozen dough to ziplock freezer bags, and store them in the freezer until the day of your party. These can be baked directly from the freezer according to the directions in each recipe.

When I suggest scooping equal portions of dough, I don't mean to imply that you should measure each cookie with a pair of calipers. But I do mean to imply that, if at all possible, you should use a cookie scoop to portion out the dough. I know I mentioned this in the Equipment Essentials section (page 25), but I think it bears repeating: These handy scoops enable you to make cookies of equal size, which means you'll have cookies that bake uniformly. This is pretty important for a cookie swap, since you're aiming for a certain number of cookies and don't want anyone to end up with the dregs of the batch.

With the right tools—and there are only a very few—drop cookies couldn't be easier to make. Which makes them a cookie swap staple: They're homey, comforting crowd pleasers, they pack and tote well, and they're an easy go-to whenever a spur-of-the-moment swap opportunity arises. I've served up my very best recipes in this chapter, including all of the beloved classics and some unusual—and uncommonly delicious—creations. I hope you and your friends will find something to love among the offerings.

Chewy Chocolate Chip Cookies

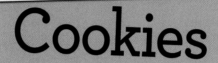

Everyone loves a good chocolate chip—and this one's the best!

MAKES:
About 48 cookies

BAKE TIME:
9 to 11 minutes

QUICK PREP

FREEZE ME!

Bringing chocolate chip cookies to a cookie exchange is a bold move: Everyone's an expert and you'll be judged by how special yours are. Not to fear—you won't go wrong with these! I've tinkered with the standard recipe to come up with my ideal: a soft, moist, chewy cookie that's rich but not greasy, with more than a hint of molasses from a high proportion of brown sugar. Melted butter is the secret to their superior texture, and also lets you bake whenever the mood strikes, since there's no time spent waiting for the butter to soften up!

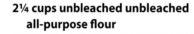

2¼ cups unbleached unbleached all-purpose flour

1 teaspoon baking soda

1 teaspoon salt

1 cup (2 sticks) unsalted butter, melted and cooled slightly

1 cup firmly packed light brown sugar

½ cup granulated sugar

2 large eggs

1 teaspoon pure vanilla extract

2 cups semisweet chocolate chips

1½ cups chopped walnuts (optional)

1. Preheat the oven to 375°F.

2. Combine the flour, baking soda, and salt in a medium bowl.

3. Place the butter and sugars in a large bowl and stir together with a wooden spoon until smooth. Add the eggs and vanilla and stir until smooth. Stir in the flour mixture until just incorporated. Stir in the chocolate chips and the nuts, if you are using them. Place the bowl in the refrigerator (no need to cover it) to let the dough firm up, for 10 minutes (or up to 6 hours).

4. Drop the batter by heaping tablespoonfuls onto ungreased baking sheets, leaving about 3 inches between each cookie. (The dough can be frozen at this point; see "A Step Ahead," right.)

5. Bake the cookies until golden around the edges but still soft on top, 9 to 11 minutes. Let the cookies stand on the baking sheet for 5 minutes and then remove them with a metal spatula to a wire rack to cool completely.

Chewy Chocolate Chip Cookies will keep in an airtight container at room temperature for 3 to 4 days.

VARIATIONS

Chocolate chip cookies definitely lend themselves to the "kitchen sink" approach. You can toss in any favorite ingredient, adding no more than 3½ cups total of chips, nuts, dried fruit, etc., so as not to overwhelm the dough. Here are some of my favorite flavor mash-ups:

Hazelnut Espresso Chip Cookies

Add 2 tablespoons of instant espresso powder to the dough along with the vanilla. Substitute 1½ cups chopped, skinned hazelnuts (see page 120) for the walnuts.

Mexican Chocolate Chip Cookies

Add 1 teaspoon of cinnamon and ⅛ teaspoon cayenne pepper to the dry ingredients.

Coconut Chocolate Chip Cookies

Reduce the granulated sugar to ¾ cup. Add 3 cups of sweetened flaked coconut along with the chocolate chips. If you like, substitute chopped, unsalted macadamia nuts for the walnuts.

Cherry-Almond Milk Chocolate Chip Cookies

Substitute chopped almonds for the walnuts, use milk chocolate chips for the semisweet chips, and add 1 cup of dried cherries to the batter along with the chips.

» A STEP AHEAD

The dropped dough can be frozen on the baking sheets, transferred to ziplock plastic freezer bags, and stored in the freezer for up to 1 month. Transfer frozen dough to ungreased baking sheets and bake a minute or two longer than directed.

Chocolate and Peppermint Bark Cookies

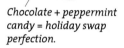

Chocolate + peppermint candy = holiday swap perfection.

MAKES: 48 cookies
BAKE TIME:
10 to 12 minutes
QUICK PREP
FREEZE ME!

For some reason, crushed peppermint candy on its own just disappears into cookie dough, whereas peppermint embedded in shards of dark chocolate retains its shape and consistency during baking, making it a great holiday addition to these truffle-like cookies. As Christmas approaches, Williams-Sonoma and other specialty shops slash their prices on gift boxes filled with delicious peppermint bark. That's when I swoop in, grab up as much as I can carry, and bake batches of these cookies to give or swap. Peppermint bark is also often available at a good price and in large quantities at warehouse clubs such as Costco and gourmet discounters such a Trader Joe's.

4 ounces unsweetened chocolate, finely chopped

8 ounces semisweet or bittersweet chocolate, finely chopped

½ cup (1 stick) unsalted butter, cut into pieces

½ cup unbleached unbleached all-purpose flour

½ teaspoon baking powder

½ teaspoon salt

4 large eggs

1½ cups sugar

1½ teaspoons pure vanilla extract

1½ cups chopped peppermint bark (white and/or dark chocolate bark)

1. Preheat the oven to 350°F. Line several baking sheets with parchment paper.

2. Put water to a depth of 1 inch in the bottom of a double boiler or medium saucepan set over low heat and bring to a bare simmer. Combine the unsweetened chocolate, semisweet chocolate, and the butter in the top of the double boiler or in a stainless-steel bowl set on top of the simmering water, making sure that the water doesn't touch the bottom of the bowl. Heat, whisking occasionally, until the chocolate and butter are completely melted. Set aside to cool slightly.

3. Combine the flour, baking powder, and salt in a small bowl.

4. Place the eggs and sugar in a large bowl and beat with an electric mixer on high until they are thick and pale, about 5 minutes. Add the chocolate mixture and vanilla and beat on low until smooth. Add the flour mixture and beat until just combined. Stir in the peppermint bark. Place the bowl, uncovered, in the refrigerator to let the dough firm up, for 15 minutes (or up to 6 hours).

•

5. Drop the dough by heaping tablespoonfuls onto the prepared baking sheets, leaving about 3 inches between each cookie. (The dough can be frozen at this point; see "A Step Ahead," right.)

6. Bake the cookies until the tops are cracked and shiny, 10 to 12 minutes. Carefully slide the parchment paper with the cookies to a wire rack and let the cookies cool completely.

Chocolate and Peppermint Bark Cookies will keep in an airtight container at room temperature for 3 to 4 days.

VARIATIONS

Chocolate Chocolate Chip Cookies

If you are in search of a great chocolate chocolate chip cookie recipe, look no further—this recipe is easily adaptable to the chocoholic's needs. Simply substitute 1½ cups of chocolate chips for the peppermint bark. Use Ghirardelli brand 60% Cacao Bittersweet Chips and you will get a rich truffle-like cookie.

Chocolate Polka-Dot Cookies

Substitute 1½ cups of white chocolate chips for the peppermint bark to get a fun black-and-white effect.

>> **A STEP AHEAD**

The dropped dough can be frozen on the baking sheets, transferred to ziplock plastic freezer bags, and stored in the freezer for up to 1 month. Transfer the frozen dough to parchment-lined baking sheets and bake a minute or two longer than directed.

Party On

A Win-Win // CHOCOLATE CHIP COOKIE BAKE-OFF!

Is there anyone who doesn't love chocolate chip cookies? I'm willing to bet that anybody with an oven has baked a batch at one time or another. And when it comes to these classics, even the meekest bakers crow about how perfectly chewy/crispy/chocolaty/buttery/fill-in-the-blank their cookies are. Since everyone's an expert, why not challenge your guests to bring their A-game at a cookie bake-off?!

Keep the guest list to six or so—more than a half dozen types of chocolate chip cookie might test the affection of even the most devoted fan. And on the off chance that your guests don't have a favorite recipe of their own, you can try mixing it up by asking them to bake chocolate chippers in a variety of shapes, flavors, and styles (drop, bar, slice-and-bake, biscotti, and so on). Lastly, if your guests are local, hand deliver their invitations and include a bag of semisweet, white, or milk chocolate morsels to get them started.

Beverages can be simple. Serve ice-cold pitchers of milk for the kids-and-parents set. For an adults-only crowd, set out some oloroso sherry; the nutty-sweet fortified wine pairs just as well with chocolate chip cookies as it does with savory snacks such as spiced nuts, olives, and salamis.

Gingerbread Chocolate Chip Cookies

Ginger and chocolate, so happy together.

Ginger and chocolate? Who'd have thunk it? If you've never considered this somewhat improbable pairing, prepare yourself for cookie nirvana. This is my favorite ginger-molasses cookie, soft and chewy and studded with milk chocolate chips and nips of crystallized ginger. The combination makes for a particularly complex and well-balanced cookie, peppery and spicy because of the ginger but with a smooth, mellow flavor and gooey richness from the chocolate.

MAKES: 48 cookies
BAKE TIME: 10 to 12 minures
QUICK PREP
FREEZE ME!

2 cups unbleached unbleached all-purpose flour

1 teaspoon ground ginger

¼ teaspoon ground cinnamon

⅛ teaspoon ground cloves

½ teaspoon salt

½ teaspoon baking soda

¾ cup (1½ sticks) unsalted butter, at room temperature

¾ cup packed light brown sugar

¼ cup dark (not light or blackstrap) molasses

2 large eggs

2 cups milk chocolate chips

½ cup finely chopped crystallized ginger (see Note)

1. Preheat the oven to 350°F. Line several baking sheets with parchment paper.

2. Combine the flour, ginger, cinnamon, cloves, salt, and baking soda in a medium bowl.

3. Place the butter, sugar, and molasses in a large bowl and beat together with an electric mixer on medium until smooth, about 3 minutes. Add the eggs and beat until smooth. Stir in the flour mixture until just combined. Stir in the chocolate chips and crystallized ginger.

SMART COOKIE

Sugar Crash CHOCOLATE CHIP COOKIE EMERGENCIES

About to bake up some chocolate chippers and realize you're missing a key ingredient? You're snowed in, your car's got a flat, and the supermarket is ten miles away? Don't know what to do? Here's what:

* **You have dark brown sugar, but no light brown sugar:** No problem—dark brown sugar will work exactly the same way as light brown sugar. There may be a slight difference in flavor (dark brown sugar will give the cookies a hint of molasses), but sweetness and texture will be unaffected.

* **You have no brown sugar:** This is a trickier one. Brown sugar (light and dark) not only adds color and a little molasses flavor to cookies, but it adds moisture, too. So if you substitute white sugar, your cookies will be less moist than cookies made with some brown sugar. If at all possible, run to the store (even convenience stores often carry brown sugar) to buy a box of brown sugar, since chocolate chip cookies get much of their character from this one ingredient. And if that's not an option, consider adding miniature chocolate chips to a shortbread or vanilla icebox cookie.

* **You have no chocolate chips:** As long as you have some other add-ins, you're in business: chopped chocolate bars, mini chocolate chips, white chocolate chips, peanut butter chips, butterscotch chips . . . you name it. I am particularly fond of chopped Lindt white and milk chocolate bars in my cookies. Just make sure you are adding the same amount as is called for in your recipe. A bag of semisweet morsels weighs about 12 ounces (and contains 2 cups of chips); other sizes and flavors of chips come in the same size bag. For chocolate chunks, you can use three 4-ounce bars (or buy four 3.5-ounce bars, chop 12 ounces, and eat the remainder!).

4. Drop the batter by heaping tablespoonfuls onto the prepared baking sheets, leaving about 3 inches between each cookie. (The dough can be frozen at this point; see "A Step Ahead," right.)

5. Bake the cookies until the edges are firm but the tops are still soft, 10 to 12 minutes. Let them stand on the baking sheet for 5 minutes and then carefully slide the parchment paper with the cookies to a wire rack and let them cool completely.

Gingerbread Chocolate Chip Cookies will keep in an airtight container at room temperature for 3 to 4 days.

Note: Crystallized ginger, also called candied ginger, can be found at most gourmet food shops and in the spice aisle at some supermarkets.

VARIATION
Molasses Raisin Cookies
Leave out the chocolate chips, stir in 1 cup of plump dark raisins or sweetened dried cranberries, and you'll have a satisfying fruit-studded molasses cookie instead of a chocolate chipper.

>> **A STEP AHEAD**
The dropped dough can be frozen on the baking sheets, then transferred to ziplock plastic freezer bags, and stored in the freezer for up to 1 month. Transfer the frozen dough to parchment-lined baking sheets and bake a minute or two longer than directed.

Classic Peanut Butter Cookies

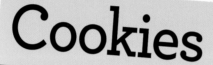

Consider these delectables for a classic cookie bake-off-meets-swap.

MAKES: 48 cookies
BAKE TIME:
15 minutes
QUICK PREP
FREEZE ME!

I like my peanut butter cookies to really taste like peanuts, so to amp up the flavor and texture, I stir in chopped, salted peanuts. Not only does this make the cookies extra peanutty, but the salt on the peanuts balances out the sweetness of the dough. Don't forget the crosshatch decoration on top—it's simple to create and gives these the classic peanut-butter–cookie look that everyone loves.

1 cup dry-roasted salted peanuts

2 cups unbleached all-purpose flour

½ teaspoon baking soda

½ teaspoon baking powder

½ teaspoon salt

1 cup (2 sticks) unsalted butter,
 at room temperature

1 cup firmly packed light brown sugar

1 cup granulated sugar

2 large eggs

1 teaspoon pure vanilla extract

1 cup smooth peanut butter (preferably
 a commercial brand, such as Jif)

1. Preheat the oven to 350°F. Line several baking sheets with parchment paper.

2. Place the nuts in a food processor and pulse 5 to 8 times to chop fine (they should look like very coarse sand).

3. Combine the flour, baking soda, baking powder, and salt in a medium bowl.

4. Place the butter and sugars in a large bowl and beat them together with an electric mixer on medium until fluffy, about 3 minutes. Add the eggs, vanilla, and peanut butter and beat until smooth. Stir in the flour mixture until just combined. Stir in the chopped peanuts.

5. Scoop the dough in heaping tablespoons, rolling each one between your palms to form a ball. Place the balls on the prepared baking sheets, leaving about 3 inches between each cookie. Press each cookie with the back of a fork twice, in opposite directions, to make a crisscross pattern. (The dough can be frozen at this point; see "A Step Ahead," right.)

6. Bake the cookies until they begin to brown slightly around the edges, about 15 minutes. Let them stand on the baking sheet for 5 minutes and then carefully slide the parchment paper with the cookies to a wire rack and let them cool completely.

Classic Peanut Butter Cookies will keep in an airtight container at room temperature for 3 to 4 days.

» A STEP AHEAD

The crosshatched dough can be frozen on the baking sheets, transferred to ziplock plastic freezer bags, and stored in the freezer for up to 1 month. Transfer the frozen dough to parchment-lined baking sheets and bake a minute or two longer than directed.

"A balanced diet is a cookie in each hand."

UNKNOWN

Double Peanut Butter Cups

MAKES: 60 cookies
BAKE TIME:
12 minutes
QUICK PREP

To create a cookie version of one of my favorite candies, I bake peanut butter cookie dough in mini-muffin tins, and when the cookies are still hot from the oven press a mini Reese's Peanut Butter Cup into each one. Seriously yummy. Be sure to use nonstick muffin tins, and don't overfill the cups or you may have trouble removing your cookies. If double peanut butter isn't your thing. Hershey's Kisses work well, too (just insert them pointy-side down).

1 recipe Classic Peanut Butter Cookie dough (page 40)

48 mini Reese's Peanut Butter Cups, unwrapped

1. Preheat the oven to 375°F.

2. Shape the dough into balls using a tablespoon-size cookie scoop and place the balls into ungreased mini-muffin tins.

3. Bake the cookies until they are just firm, about 12 minutes.

4. Remove the tins from the oven to wire racks. Immediately press a peanut butter cup, right side up, into each cookie so the top of the peanut butter cup is almost flush with the top of the cookie. Let the cookies cool in the tins completely before carefully removing them.

Double Peanut Butter Cups will keep in an airtight container at room temperature for 3 to 4 days.

Nut-and-Jam Thumbprints

Put your "print" on these cookies with your choice of nuts and jam.

You can use any combination of chopped nuts and jam that you like for these classic thumbprints. I like to pair almonds with apricot, pecans with blueberry, walnuts with raspberry, and hazelnuts with orange marmalade. For a chocolate-hazelnut version (filled with Nutella instead of jam), see the variation that follows.

MAKES:
48 small cookies
BAKE TIME:
15 to 18 minutes
QUICK PREP
FREEZE ME!

1½ cups whole almonds, skinned hazelnuts, pecan halves, or walnut pieces

2 cups unbleached all-purpose flour

½ teaspoon salt

1 cup (2 sticks) unsalted butter, at room temperature

½ cup firmly packed light brown sugar

6 tablespoons granulated sugar

1 large egg

1 teaspoon pure vanilla extract

½ cup best-quality jam of your choice (see headnote)

1. Preheat the oven to 325°F. Line several baking sheets with parchment paper.

2. Place the nuts in a food processor and pulse 5 to 8 times to chop fine (they should look like very coarse sand). Combine the flour, salt, and chopped nuts in a medium bowl.

3. Place the butter and sugars in a large bowl and beat together with an electric mixer on medium-high until fluffy, 2 to 3 minutes. Add the egg and vanilla extract and beat on low until

≫ A STEP AHEAD

The rolled dough can be frozen on the baking sheets, transferred to ziplock plastic freezer bags, and stored in the freezer for up to 1 month. Defrost the dough for 10 minutes on parchment-lined baking sheets before making the "thumbprints" and proceeding as directed.

smooth. Stir in the flour mixture until just combined.

4. Scoop the dough in scant tablespoonfuls, rolling each between your palms to form a ball. Place the balls on the prepared baking sheets, leaving about 2 inches between each cookie. (The dough can be frozen at this point; see "A Step Ahead," left.) Press each cookie with the back of a small measuring spoon to make a "thumbprint" in the center.

5. Bake the cookies until they are golden around the edges, 15 to 18 minutes. Let them stand on the baking sheet for 5 minutes and then carefully slide the parchment paper with the cookies to a wire rack and let them cool completely.

6. When the cookies are cool, fill each thumbprint with ½ teaspoon jam.

Nut-and-Jam Thumbprints will keep, layered between parchment paper, in an airtight container at room temperature for 3 to 4 days.

SMART COOKIE

Seeds of Change
HOW TO SEED JAM

If your recipe calls for seedless jam, and you only have jam with seeds, simply press your jam through a fine mesh strainer to remove the seeds. You'll need to start out with more jam than the recipe calls for since seeds take up substantial volume, so remember to measure the jam again *after* seeding it.

VARIATION
Nutella-Filled Chocolate Hazelnut Thumbprints

Reduce the flour to 1½ cups and add ½ cup sifted unsweetened cocoa powder to the dry ingredients; proceed as directed. Spoon (or use a pastry bag to pipe) ½ teaspoon of Nutella into each thumbprint after the baked cookies have cooled.

Classic Oatmeal Raisin Cookies

Here's my favorite oatmeal cookie recipe, studded with raisins for sweetness and spiced with cinnamon and cloves for depth of flavor. Use fresh, plump raisins from a just-opened box so they stay moist during baking.

MAKES: 48 cookies
BAKE TIME:
15 to 17 minutes
QUICK PREP
FREEZE ME!

1½ cups unbleached all-purpose flour

1 teaspoon baking soda

½ teaspoon salt

½ teaspoon cinnamon

⅛ teaspoon ground cloves

1 cup (2 sticks) unsalted butter, melted and cooled slightly

1 cup firmly packed light brown sugar

½ cup granulated sugar

2 large eggs

1 teaspoon pure vanilla extract

3 cups rolled oats (not instant)

1½ cups raisins

1. Preheat the oven to 350°F.

2. Combine the flour, baking soda, salt, cinnamon, and cloves in a medium bowl.

3. Place the melted butter and sugars in a large bowl and beat together with an electric mixer on medium until smooth. Add the eggs and vanilla, and beat until well blended. Stir in the flour mixture until just combined. Stir in the oats and raisins. Place the bowl in the refrigerator, uncovered, to let the dough firm up, for 10 minutes (or up to 6 hours).

>> A STEP AHEAD

The dropped dough can be frozen on baking sheets, then, transferred to ziplock plastic freezer bags, and stored in the freezer for up to 1 month. Transfer the frozen dough to ungreased cookie sheets and bake a minute or two longer than directed.

4. Drop the batter by heaping tablespoonfuls onto ungreased baking sheets, leaving about 3 inches between each cookie. (The dough can be frozen at this point; see "A Step Ahead," left.)

5. Bake the cookies until they are golden around the edges but still soft on top, 15 to 17 minutes. Let them stand on the baking sheet for 5 minutes and then remove them with a metal spatula to a wire rack to cool completely.

Classic Oatmeal Raisin Cookies will keep in an airtight container at room temperature for 3 to 4 days.

VARIATION
Cranberry-Orange Oatmeal Cookies with White Chocolate Drizzle

With a few simple twists you can turn wholesome oatmeal cookies into something snazzier: Omit the cinnamon, add 2 teaspoons of orange zest in step 3, and replace the raisins with 1½ cups sweetened dried cranberries and 1½ cups chopped walnuts, almonds, or pecans. Proceed with the recipe as directed. Transfer the cooled cookies to parchment-lined baking sheets.

Place 1 cup white chocolate chips in a microwave-safe bowl and microwave uncovered on high until almost melted, 30 seconds to 1 minute. (Alternatively, melt them in a double boiler; see "Control Your Temper," page 94.) Stir until smooth. Transfer the chocolate to a medium ziplock bag. Snip a small hole in one corner of the bag and, holding it as you would a pastry bag, pipe free-form lines onto the cookies. Let the chocolate harden, about 30 minutes. (If you prefer, you can stir in the white chocolate chips with the cranberries and nuts in Step 3.)

Oatmeal cookies get a makeover in this elegantly adorned variation.

Chewy
Gingersnaps

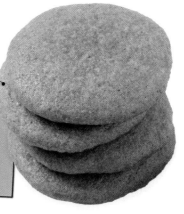

Comfort food in cookie form, made for an autumn swap.

I t's not really fair to call these "snaps" since they have the appealingly toothsome chew of my favorite molasses cookie. But they do have the wonderful spicy flavor of gingersnaps, so I figure we can bend the rules a little, just this once.

MAKES: 36 cookies
BAKE TIME: 10 minutes
QUICK PREP
FREEZE ME!

2 cups unbleached all-purpose flour

1½ teaspoons ground ginger

½ teaspoon ground cinnamon

¼ teaspoon ground cloves

½ teaspoon salt

½ teaspoon baking soda

¾ cup (1½ sticks) unsalted butter, melted and cooled

1 cup sugar

¼ cup dark (not light or blackstrap) molasses

2 large eggs

1. Preheat the oven to 350°F. Line several baking sheets with parchment paper.

2. Combine the flour, ginger, cinnamon, cloves, salt, and baking soda in a medium bowl.

3. Place the butter, sugar, and molasses in a large bowl and stir together with a wooden spoon until smooth. Add the eggs and beat with an electric mixer on low until smooth. Stir in the flour mixture until just incorporated. Place the bowl in the refrigerator, uncovered, to let the dough firm up, about 10 minutes.

4. Drop the batter by tablespoonfuls onto the parchment-lined baking sheets, leaving at least 2 inches between each cookie. (The dough can be frozen at this point; see "A Step Ahead," left.)

5. Bake the cookies until they are firm around the edges but still soft on top, about 10 minutes. Let them stand on the baking sheet for 5 minutes, and then slide the parchment with the cookies to a wire rack to cool completely.

Chewy Gingersnaps will keep in an airtight container at room temperature for 3 to 4 days.

Fall for Fall // AUTUMN HARVEST COOKIE SWAP

Every September I pile my family into the car and we head out to a nearby apple orchard, where we pick a dozen varieties of locally grown fruit. We always come home with more apples than we can eat. Next time this happens, I'm going to set them out at a cookie swap, right in their attractive white paper sacks, for everyone to enjoy. I'll put out hunks of cheddar cheese with crackers. A big pot of apple cider (page 209) warming on the stovetop will perfume the air. Cookie suggestions? Anything autumnal, with dried fruit and/or nuts, would fit the bill, but Chewy Gingersnaps or wholesome Classic Oatmeal Raisin Cookies (page 45) are my top picks. For take-out containers, offer small baskets padded with colorful fall leaves (the cookies can be wrapped in tissue paper and placed on top).

Very Vanilla Sprinkle Cookies

These blank canvas cookies can be decorated to fit almost any occasion.

This is a great recipe for kids and grown-ups who like their cookies bright and festive but subtly flavored: They're tender vanilla cookies glazed with a vanilla icing and bedecked with rainbow sprinkles or nonpareils. I like the graphic look of the cookies when they're only half-covered with sprinkles, leaving the other half snowy white with icing. If you're not in a rainbow mood, tailor your sprinkle to the occasion: green for St. Patrick's Day; red, white, and blue for the Fourth of July; pink, blue, or pastels for a baby shower.

MAKES: 48 cookies
BAKE TIME: 11 to 14 minutes
FREEZE ME!

FOR THE COOKIES

Nonstick cooking spray (optional)

4 cups unbleached all-purpose flour

2 teaspoon baking powder

1 teaspoon baking soda

½ teaspoon salt

1 cup (2 sticks) unsalted butter, at room temperature

1¾ cups sugar

2 large eggs

1 tablespoon pure vanilla extract

1 cup sour cream

FOR THE DECORATION

⅔ cup colored sprinkles or nonpareils

2 cups confectioners' sugar

⅓ cup heavy cream, plus more if necessary

1½ teaspoons pure vanilla extract

1. Preheat the oven to 350°F. Line several baking sheets with parchment paper or spray them with nonstick cooking spray.

>> **A STEP AHEAD**
The dropped dough can be frozen on the baking sheets, transferred to ziplock plastic freezer bags, and stored in the freezer for up to 1 month. Frozen dough should be placed on parchment-lined baking sheets and defrosted for 10 minutes before flattening the cookies and proceeding as directed.

2. Make the cookies: Combine the flour, baking powder, baking soda, and salt in a medium bowl.

3. Place the butter and sugar in a large bowl and beat with an electric mixer on medium until well-combined, scraping down the sides of the bowl once or twice as necessary, 2 to 3 minutes.

4. Add the eggs and vanilla and beat on medium until combined. Beat in half of the flour mixture on low until just incorporated. Beat in the sour cream. Beat in the remaining flour mixture until just combined.

5. Use a small ice-cream scoop or heaping tablespoonful to drop mounds of dough 3 inches apart onto the baking sheets. (The dough can be frozen at this point; see "A Step Ahead," left.) With moistened palms, flatten the mounds into 1½-inch-thick disks.

6. Bake the cookies until the centers are firm and the edges are just lightly golden, 11 to 14 minutes. Cool for 5 minutes on the baking sheets and then carefully slide the parchment paper with the cookies to a wire rack and let them cool completely.

7. Make the decoration: Place the sprinkles in a shallow bowl. To make the icing, put the confectioners' sugar, the ⅓ cup of cream, and the vanilla in a small bowl and whisk together until smooth. (The icing should be loose enough to spread with a spatula, but not so loose that it runs off of the cookies; add more cream if necessary, until the proper consistency is reached.)

8. With a small metal offset spatula, spread the icing over each cookie. Working over the bowl, scatter the sprinkles heavily over half of each cookie, letting extra sprinkles fall back into the bowl. Let the cookies stand until the icing is set, about 30 minutes.

Very Vanilla Sprinkle Cookies will keep, layered between parchment paper in an airtight container at room temperature for up to 3 days.

From-Scratch Amaretti

The Sophia Loren of cookies; offer these sophisticated treats at an Italy-themed swap.

These cookies, made with ground almonds, are more rustic and less sweet than commercial amaretti, which are made with almond paste. In Italy, these rather grown-up cookies are served with a sweet dessert wine such as vin santo or a selection of after-dinner liqueurs. Serve them this way at your party, perhaps along with a generous antipasti selection. *Viva Italia!*

MAKES: 48 cookies
BAKE TIME:
14 to 16 minutes
QUICK PREP
FREEZE ME!

2⅔ cups (14 ounces) whole almonds

2 cups sugar

½ cup unbleached all-purpose flour

¼ teaspoon salt

4 large egg whites

1 teaspoon pure vanilla extract

1 teaspoon pure almond extract

1. Preheat the oven to 350°F. Line several baking sheets with parchment paper.

2. Place the almonds and ½ cup sugar in a food processor and pulse 5 to 8 times to chop fine (the mixture should look like very coarse sand). Add the remaining sugar, flour, and salt, and pulse several times to combine.

3. Transfer the almond mixture to a large bowl and add the egg whites, vanilla, and almond extracts. Beat with an electric mixer on medium until thoroughly combined, stopping once or twice to scrape down the sides of the bowl.

>> A STEP AHEAD

The shaped dough can be frozen on the baking sheets, transferred to ziplock plastic freezer bags, and stored in the freezer for up to 1 month. Transfer the frozen dough to parchment-lined baking sheets and and bake a minute or two longer than directed.

4. With moistened hands, roll tablespoonfuls of the dough into balls and place them on the prepared cookie sheets, at least 2 inches apart. If you have any leftover dough, set it aside. (The dough can be frozen at this point; see "A Step Ahead," left.)

5. Bake the cookies until they are lightly golden, 14 to 16 minutes.

6. Let the cookies stand on the baking sheets for 5 minutes and then carefully slide the parchment paper with the cookies to wire racks; let the cookies cool completely. Repeat from Step 3 with any remaining dough.

From-Scratch Amaretti will keep in an airtight container at room temperature for 3 to 4 days.

Cinnamon Paradiso // COOKIE SWAP *AL ITALIA*

Break out the Chianti and bake up some cookies: It's time for an Italian cookie exchange! Deck out your space in red, white, and green and ask your friends to bring cookies inspired by Italy, such as From-Scratch Amaretti, biscotti (pages 149–158), Florentines, pine nut cookies, or even Rolled Vanilla Cookies with Royal Icing (page 136)—cut into the shape of the boot, of course. Provide takeout pizza or pasta, platters of antipasti, Italian wines, and a few bottles of Pellegrino to fuel your swappers. A soundtrack of Verdi, Puccini, Donizetti, and Rossini would set the mood, but if opera isn't your thing, go to www.italianpop.com for help in putting together a playlist. For favors, hand out pizza key chains (available at carnivalsource.com) and small bottles of olive oil. *Perfetto*.

Chapter 4

RAISE THE BAR

SUPERIOR BROWNIES, BLONDIES, AND BARS

Anyone seeking to win brownie points at their next swap has come to the right place. Luscious, gooey, and satisfyingly chewy, brownies and bars are often the most popular guests at an exchange. These chameleon cookies adapt to please chocolate and vanilla lovers alike; they tempt fans of nut, spice, citrus, and everything in between. In short, bar cookies offer something for everyone—including the baker.

That's because bar cookies are great time-savers. The time-pressed baker can simply scrape dough into a pan and pop it into the oven. Even bars with double layers, such as pecan bars, require less total work and baking time than a batch of chocolate chip cookies. And most are sturdy enough to transport across town without breakage.

You can also whip up a batch of bars days or weeks before your swap. Simply freeze the baked bars once they've cooled: Pull the uncut bars from the pan, peel away the foil, then wrap the bars in two layers of plastic and one layer of foil, and store them in the freezer (see individual recipes for specific instructions). The day before the party, let the bars defrost overnight in the refrigerator, cut them with a sharp chef's knife (cut down, not in a sawing motion), and store them in an airtight container.

Although bar cookies are exceedingly easy to make, there is a chance they'll bake unevenly when in a large pan. To avoid bars that are too dry at the edges but still raw in the center, pull the cookies from the oven a couple of minutes before you think the center is fully baked. The batter will continue to set up as the bars cool (and you can take heart knowing some people prefer their bars gooey and others cakey). I recommend using metal pans for these recipes; although glass pans will work, bars baked in them will cook more quickly (and thus can burn if not watched).

The bar cookie recipes that follow are sure to tempt at your next swap. The Incredibly Fudgy Brownies just might be the best you've ever tasted (bring the recipe with you—people will request it), and you'll also find scrumptious blondies and delectable fruit-laced and nut-filled bars. They're some of my absolute favorites—bar none.

Incredibly Fudgy Brownies

Melt-in-your mouth rich and deeply chocolate, these are the ne plus ultra of brownies.

I've been wanting to develop a fudgy truffle-like brownie for years, and working on this book gave me the perfect opportunity to try out a few different approaches. When I came up with these moist bars, I knew I'd hit the jackpot. They are dark and dense in the extreme. They're an ideal cookie swap choice because they stay fresh longer than cakey brownies.

MAKES: 36 brownies
BAKE TIME: 30 to 35 minutes
QUICK PREP
FREEZE ME!

4 ounces unsweetened chocolate, finely chopped

1½ cups semisweet or bittersweet chocolate chips

½ cup (1 stick) unsalted butter, cut into pieces

½ cup unbleached all-purpose flour

2 teaspoons instant espresso powder

¼ teaspoon baking powder

½ teaspoon salt

4 large eggs

1½ cups sugar

2 teaspoons pure vanilla extract

1. Preheat the oven to 350°F. Line a 9-by-13-inch baking pan with heavy-duty aluminum foil, making sure the foil is tucked into all the corners and there is at least 1 inch overhanging the top of the pan on all sides.

2. Put water to a depth of 1 inch in the bottom of a double boiler or

>> **A STEP AHEAD**

Remove the cooled, uncut bars from the pan by grasping the overhanging foil and pulling it up. Peel away the foil and wrap the bars in a double layer of plastic and then a layer of heavy-duty foil. Freeze for up to 2 weeks. Defrost on the countertop for several hours before cutting into bars.

medium saucepan set over low heat and bring to a bare simmer. Combine the unsweetened chocolate, chocolate chips, and butter in the top of the double boiler or in a stainless steel bowl set on top of the simmering water, making sure that the water doesn't touch the bottom of the bowl. Heat, whisking occasionally, until the chocolate and butter are completely melted. Set aside to cool slightly.

3. Combine the flour, espresso powder, baking powder, and salt in a small bowl.

4. Place the eggs and sugar in a large bowl and whisk together until the mixture is pale yellow and slightly increased in volume, 2 to 3 minutes. Stir in the chocolate mixture and vanilla. Stir in the flour mixture until just combined.

5. Pour the batter into the prepared pan. Bake the brownies until they are just set and a few moist crumbs stick to a toothpick inserted into the center, 30 to 35 minutes. Set the pan on a wire rack and let the brownies cool completely. (The brownies can be frozen at this point; see "A Step Ahead," left.)

6. Grasping the overhanging foil on either side of the pan, lift out the brownies and place them on a cutting board. Place the board in the freezer for 10 minutes, to allow the brownies to firm up. Slice the brownies into 36 pieces, and peel them from the foil.

Incredibly Fudgy Brownies will keep in an airtight container at room temperature for 3 to 4 days.

Ganache-Glazed Brownie Bites

Sweet and lovely treats for any sweet and lovely swap occasion, such as a baby shower or bridal shower.

Spooning brownie batter into mini baking cups allows you to make 48 little brownie cakes (a higher yield than you'll get with a 9-by-13-inch baking dish). These bitty bites are not only cute, but also pretty: Each one is dressed up with a spoonful of rich ganache on top and a candied violet or whimsical sugar decoration.

MAKES: 48 brownies
BAKE TIME:
12 to 15 minutes

1 recipe Incredibly Fudgy Brownie batter (page 55)

2 ounces bittersweet chocolate, finely chopped (about ⅓ cup)

¼ cup heavy cream

Candied violets or sugar decorations (optional; see Resources, page 216)

1. Preheat the oven to 350°F. Line 48 mini-muffin cups with paper liners and set the pans on baking sheets.

2. Fill each cup about three quarters full with batter. Bake until the brownie tops are shiny and cracked, 12 to 15 minutes. Transfer the muffin pans to wire racks and let the brownies cool completely. Remove the cooled brownies from the cups and place them on a wire rack set over a baking sheet.

3. Place the chocolate in a small heat-proof bowl. Bring the cream to a boil in a small saucepan over

medium-high heat. Pour the cream over the chocolate, cover the bowl with plastic wrap, and let stand until the chocolate is melted, about 5 minutes. Whisk until smooth. Let the glaze stand at room temperature until it thickens slightly, about 30 minutes.

4. With a small metal spatula, spread a little glaze over each brownie and let stand at room temperature until the glaze sets up, about 2 hours. Top each brownie with a candied violet, if desired.

Ganache-Glazed Brownie Bites will keep, layered between parchment paper, in an airtight container at room temperature for 3 to 4 days.

Swap Meet // VALENTINE'S DAY COOKIE MIXER

There's no reason why a cookie swap can't be an occasion for some neighborly matchmaking. Invite unattached friends for a Valentine's Day get-together and ask them to bring their most romantic cookies (heart-, rose-, and angel-shaped cookie cutters come in especially handy here). Serve sparkling wine along with some luxury appetizers: Smoked salmon on toast points, figs stuffed with goat cheese, and caviar-stuffed mini potatoes would all fit the bill (or, if you want to go all out, roll up your sleeves and shuck some oysters). Light some candles, put on some get-in-the-mood music (iTunes has several playlists, or buy a romantic jazz compilation like

Blue Valentines—From Blue Note with Love) . . . and see what happens. People may end up swapping digits along with their cookies!

What to bake? Chocolate is a given, so Ganache-Glazed Brownie Bites should be on the list. You might also consider Raspberry Meringue Kisses (page 163), Mini Hazelnut Linzer Hearts (page 118), and Maple-Walnut Wedding Cakes (page 129).

When your guests leave (in pairs, hopefully) give out goody bags filled with heart-shaped cookie cutters, Red Hots, Baci chocolates, conversation hearts, and forget-me-not seed packets (available at www.american meadows.com).

Pumpkin Cheesecake Brownies

Satisfy spice and chocolate cravings in a single bite.

I love the flavor of these brownies: The tangy, subtly spiced pumpkin cheesecake mixture is a great foil for the rich, dark chocolate. And they look pretty spiffy, too—the abstract-art layers of golden orange and deep brown make them a natural addition to any autumn swap table.

MAKES: 36 brownies
BAKE TIME: 50 to 55 minutes
FREEZE ME!

FOR THE BROWNIE BATTER

- ½ cup (1 stick) unsalted butter
- 4 ounces (4 squares) unsweetened chocolate
- ⅔ cup unbleached all-purpose flour
- ½ teaspoon baking powder
- ¼ teaspoon salt
- 1½ cups sugar
- 2 large eggs
- 1 teaspoon pure vanilla extract

FOR THE CHEESECAKE LAYER

- 2 packages (8 ounces each) cream cheese, at room temperature
- ½ cup sugar
- 2 large eggs
- 1 teaspoon pure vanilla extract
- ½ cup canned pumpkin puree
- ¼ teaspoon ground nutmeg
- ¼ teaspoon salt
- 1 tablespoon unbleached all-purpose flour

1. Preheat the oven to 325°F. Place an oven rack in the bottom third of the oven. Line a 9-by-13-inch baking pan with heavy-duty aluminum foil, making sure that the foil is tucked into all the corners and that there is at least 1 inch overhanging the top of the pan on all sides.

2. Make the brownie batter: Put water to a depth of 1 inch in the bottom of a double boiler or medium saucepan set over low heat and bring to a bare simmer. Combine the butter and chocolate in the top of the double boiler or in a stainless steel bowl and set it on top of the simmering water, making sure that the water doesn't touch the bottom of the bowl. Heat, whisking occasionally, until the butter

and chocolate are completely melted. Set aside to cool slightly.

3. Combine the flour, baking powder, and salt in a small bowl.

4. Place the sugar and eggs in a large bowl and whisk them together until combined. With a wooden spoon, stir in the chocolate mixture and the vanilla. Stir in the flour mixture until just incorporated. Spread into the prepared pan in an even layer.

5. Make the cheesecake layer: Put the cream cheese and sugar in a medium bowl and beat together with an electric mixer on medium-high until very smooth. Add the eggs and vanilla and beat again until smooth. Reduce the speed to low and beat in the pumpkin, nutmeg, salt, and flour.

6. Drop the cream cheese mixture by heaping tablespoonfuls over the brownie batter and smooth it with a rubber spatula to create an even layer.

7. Bake the brownies in the bottom third of the oven until they are set around the edges but still a little wobbly in the center, 50 to 55

minutes. Let them cool completely on a wire rack.

8. Refrigerate the brownies, covered, until they are completely chilled, at least 6 hours. (The brownies can be frozen at this point; see "A Step Ahead," right.) Just before serving, grasp the overhanging foil on either side of the pan, lift out the brownies and place

them on a cutting board. Run a sharp chef's knife under hot water, wipe it dry, and use it to cut the brownies into 36 pieces; peel the brownies from the foil.

Pumpkin Cheesecake Brownies will keep, layered beween parchment paper, in an airtight container in the refrigerator for up to 5 days.

>> A STEP AHEAD

Remove the cooled, uncut bars from the pan by grasping the overhanging foil and pulling it up. Peel away the foil and wrap the bars in a double layer of plastic and then a layer of heavy-duty foil. Freeze for up to 2 weeks. Defrost on the countertop for several hours (they should be chilled but not frozen solid) before cutting into bars.

SMART COOKIE

They Call It Pumpkin Love LEFTOVER PUMPKIN PUREE

You have a cup or so of pumpkin puree leftover from your Pumpkin Cheesecake Brownie baking. Don't throw it away. Use it to make:

* **Pumpkin-Apple Butter:** In a heavy saucepan over low heat, cook the puree with a peeled, cored, grated apple, a tablespoon or two of brown sugar, and a pinch of cinnamon until it's nice and thick, about 35 minutes. Store it in the fridge for up to 3 days and use it as a spread on toast or muffins.

* **Pumpkin Peanut Butter:** Lighten up peanut butter by mixing an equivalent

amount of pumpkin puree into it. Then use it on sandwiches with sliced bananas or apples (it will keep in the refrigerator for up to 3 days).

* **Pumpkin Mousse:** Cook a cup of pumpkin puree with ¼ cup of brown sugar and some pumpkin pie spice over low heat until the sugar is melted. Let it cool and gently fold it together with two cups of sweetened whipped cream.

My Go-to Blondies

Everyone loves a good blondie. Dress these up or down for a variety of swaps.

MAKES: 36 blondies
BAKE TIME:
25 to 30 minutes
QUICK PREP
FREEZE ME!

This is a recipe that I could turn to if I had almost no ingredients in the house and remembered I was due at a cookie swap in an hour. It's that simple. But I often turn to it when I have plenty of time and the pantry's fully stocked—these chewy, moist, brown sugar bars are just plain delicious!

2 cups unbleached all-purpose flour

2 teaspoons baking powder

½ teaspoon salt

1 cup (2 sticks) unsalted butter

2 cups firmly packed dark brown sugar

2 large eggs

2 teaspoons pure vanilla extract

1½ cups chopped walnuts (optional)

1. Preheat the oven to 350°F. Line a 9-by-13-inch baking pan with heavy-duty aluminum foil, making sure that the foil is tucked into all the corners and that there is at least 1 inch overhanging the top of the pan on all sides.

2. Combine the flour, baking powder, and salt in a small bowl.

3. Melt the butter in a medium saucepan over low heat. Remove it from the heat and stir in the brown sugar until it is dissolved. Transfer the

butter mixture to a large bowl and stir in the eggs and vanilla. Stir in the flour mixture until just incorporated. Stir in the walnuts if desired.

4. Pour the batter into the prepared baking pan. Bake the blondies until they are just set in the center, 25 to 30 minutes. Let them cool completely in the pan on a wire rack. (The blondies can be frozen at this point; see "A Step Ahead," right.)

5. Grasping the overhanging foil on either side of the pan, lift out the blondies and place them on a cutting board. Cut them into 36 pieces and peel them from the foil.

My Go-to Blondies will keep in an airtight container at room temperature for 3 to 4 days.

VARIATIONS

This is an endlessly adaptable recipe. You can pretty much stir in 2½ to 3 cups of any ingredient you like to make *your* go-to blondies. Here are a few suggestions:

Chocolate Coconut Blondies

At the end of Step 3, stir in 2 cups of chocolate chips and ¾ cup of unsweetened dried coconut. Reduce the nuts to ¾ cup.

White Chocolate and Apricot Blondies

Stir in ¾ cup of white chocolate chips and ¾ cup of chopped dried apricots. Reduce the nuts to ¾ cup.

Espresso Blondies

Stir in 2 tablespoons of instant espresso powder with the vanilla.

S'mores Blondies

At the end of Step 3, stir in 2 cups of mini marshmallows and 1 cup of semisweet chocolate chips. Reduce the nuts to ¾ cup or omit them altogether.

>> **A STEP AHEAD**

Remove the cooled, uncut bars from the pan by grasping the overhanging foil and pulling it up. Peel away the foil and wrap the bars in a double layer of plastic and then a layer of heavy-duty foil. Freeze for up to 2 weeks. Defrost on the countertop for several hours before cutting into bars.

THE DECONSTRUCTED COOKIE JAR :: A GIFT TO GO

This year, ditch the fireflies and put a new delight in your jars: cookies! The Deconstructed Cookie Jar is a perfect party favor—the gift of warm cookies whenever the mood strikes. What's a Deconstructed Cookie Jar, you ask? It's simple: Layers of dry cookie ingredients are placed in a jar, and the directions for adding wet ingredients and baking the cookies are attached. With a shelf life of several weeks, these are ideal gifts for those friends who still insist on buying rolls of refrigerated cookie dough. And they're a good bet, too, for those people who already have everything else.

Many recipes can be adapted for this purpose, particularly those that call for combining the dry ingredients before mixing them with the wet. Simple drop and bar cookies with few liquid ingredients work best, because eventually all ingredients get mixed together, anyway. (Avoid recipes that have different layers—Pumpkin Cheesecake Brownies, for example—or one that must be mixed in stages, with the butter and sugar beaten together first and then the flour mixed in second.) I like to use my Go-to Blondies, because melted butter, vanilla, and eggs are the only liquid additions.

Pack the dry ingredients in a jar of your choice. Mason jars, kitchen-storage containers, vases with cork stoppers—all are inexpensive, easy-to-come-by vessels that can be repurposed in your recipient's kitchen. If the container is see-through (recommended!), make attractive layers of dry ingredients so that your creation looks like a masterpiece of sand art. Design a tag with abridged instructions, and attach it with decorative ribbon or yarn. A cute goody like a measuring scoop or a wee butter mold make a precious addition to your gift; if you like, go ahead and loop one into the ribbon. Just make sure not to poke holes in the lid!

ButterScotch Blondies

These grown-up blondies have a secret—they're laced with Scotch.

When the occasion calls for black tie and you want a cookie to match, make these sophisticated blondies. They're spiked with Scotch whiskey, which adds a smoky undertone, and studded with creamy butterscotch chips. I like the way chopped nuts cut the sweetness of the chips, but you can skip them if you're not nuts about nuts.

MAKES: 36 blondies
BAKE TIME:
25 to 30 minutes
QUICK PREP
FREEZE ME!

2 cups plus 2 tablespoons unbleached all-purpose flour

2 teaspoons baking powder

1 teaspoon salt

1 cup (2 sticks) unsalted butter

2 cups firmly packed light brown sugar

2 large eggs

2 teaspoons pure vanilla extract

½ cup Scotch whiskey

2 cups butterscotch chips

1½ cups chopped walnuts (optional)

1. Preheat the oven to 350°F. Line a 9-by-13-inch baking pan with heavy-duty aluminum foil, making sure that the foil is tucked into all the corners and that there is at least 1 inch overhanging the top of the pan on all sides.

2. Combine the flour, baking powder, and salt in a small mixing bowl.

3. Melt the butter in a medium saucepan over low heat. Remove it from

>> A STEP AHEAD

Remove the cooled, uncut bars from the pan by grasping the overhanging foil and pulling it up. Peel away the foil and wrap the bars in a double layer of plastic and then a layer of heavy-duty foil. Freeze for up to 2 weeks. Defrost on the countertop for several hours before cutting into bars.

the heat and stir in the brown sugar until it is dissolved. Transfer the butter mixture to a large bowl and stir in the eggs and vanilla. Stir in the Scotch. Stir in the flour mixture until just incorporated. Stir in the butterscotch chips and, if desired, the walnuts.

4. Pour the batter into the prepared baking pan. Bake the blondies until they are just set in the center, 25 to 30 minutes. Let them cool completely in the pan on a wire rack. (The bars can be frozen at this point; see "A Step Ahead," left.)

5. Grasping the overhanging foil on either side of the pan, lift out the blondies and place them on a cutting board. Cut them into 36 pieces and peel them from the foil.

    ButterScotch Blondies will keep in an airtight container at room temperature for 3 to 4 days.

RECIPES FOR SUCCESS — COOKIE SWAP PARTY GAMES

Since you're already the perfect host, you know that games are sure to keep any party going. One way to stir a dash of spice into your cookie swap is to include cookie- and-baking-themed games that keep the focus on sweets. Try one of these with a playful crowd:

Edward Mittenhands Place a gift card or other small prize inside a box and wrap the box with layer upon layer of paper (the number of layers will depend on how many people are playing and how long you want the game to last). Sit in a circle, placing a pair of cloth oven mitts next to the gift in the center. Let each person take a turn rolling a pair of dice. Whoever rolls a double puts on the oven mitts and scrambles to unwrap the gift while the dice make their way around the circle. As soon as someone else rolls a double, that person takes over the mitted unwrapping. Whoever unwraps the gift completely gets the prize. (Whether the prize is a good one or a gag gift is up to you.)

Ingredient Challenge This game is best played with unusual, distinctive cookies, or cookies that no one in your crowd has tried before. Blindfolded, two players taste a cookie, and take turns guessing its flavor ingredients (such as vanilla, molasses, star anise; skip the obvious ingredients, like flour, sugar, and butter). The contestants go back and forth until someone makes a mistake. If the other contestant can correctly name one more ingredient after his opponent has messed up, s/he wins the game. The baker of the cookie judges.

What Cookie Am I? Place a sign with the name of a cookie on the back of each party guest. Each guest must ask fellow revelers questions about which cookie they are. Hilarity ensues. A good choice for kiddie-centric cookie swaps.

Cookie Identity Crisis On a blank sheet of paper, have each guest provide three clues about their recipe or themselves, with the name of the recipe at the top. On another sheet, have guests guess who made which cookie. The prize goes to the person who has the most correct guesses. This quick quiz works well for an intimate gathering, where inside jokes often generate some laughs, and also for a group of loose acquaintances or even relative strangers, as an icebreaker.

Sweet Nothings This is just for a little laugh. Each person chooses a cookie-related word, and whispers it to a friend. The friend's job is to get someone else at the party to say the word out of context—without revealing their purpose (and without getting flustered)!

Cookie Charades Just what it sounds like. Take turns acting out the names of different cookies. Taboo and Catchphrase are other games that would easily adapt to the cookie theme.

Embrace your inner butterfingers with a game of Edward Mittenhands.

Midsummer Night's Dream Bars

MAKES: 36 bars
BAKE TIME:
25 to 30 minutes
QUICK PREP
FREEZE ME!

I don't know if **Shakespeare** had a favorite cookie, but I'm sure he would've loved these. I first made them for a cast party after our local high school's Shakespeare production, hence the name. But they're appropriate for any occasion, whenever you want to bake up a quick batch of bar cookies with just a few ingredients. They really steal the show.

8 tablespoons (1 stick) unsalted butter, melted

16 whole graham crackers, crushed (see Note)

2 cups whole almonds

1 cup semisweet chocolate chips

1 cup milk chocolate chips

3 cups sweetened flaked coconut

2 cans (7 ounces each) sweetened condensed milk

1. Preheat the oven to 325°F. Line a 9-by-13-inch baking pan with heavy-duty aluminum foil, making sure that the foil is tucked into all the corners and that there is at least 1 inch overhanging the top of the pan on all sides.

2. Combine the melted butter and crushed graham crackers in a medium bowl and stir until all the crumbs are moistened. Sprinkle the mixture across

the bottom of the pan and press with your fingertips into an even layer.

3. Place the almonds in a food processor and pulse 3 to 5 times to coarsely chop.

4. Scatter the almonds evenly over the crumbs. Layer both kinds of chocolate chips over the almonds. Sprinkle the coconut over the chocolate chips and press with the back of a large spoon to compact the ingredients. Drizzle the sweetened condensed milk over the coconut.

5. Bake until the coconut is golden, 25 to 30 minutes. Let the bars cool completely in the pan on a wire rack. (The bars can be frozen at this point; see "A Step Ahead," right.)

6. Grasping the overhanging foil on either side of the pan, lift out the bars and place them on a cutting board. Cut them into 36 pieces and peel them from the foil.

Midsummer Night's Dream Bars will keep in an airtight container at room temperature for up to 1 week.

Note: To crush the graham crackers, seal them in a ziplock plastic bag and roll a rolling pin over them until they're fine crumbs. You can do this in batches, if you like.

>> **A STEP AHEAD**
Remove the cooled, uncut bars from the pan by grasping the overhanging foil and pulling it up. Peel away the foil and wrap the bars in a double layer of plastic and then a layer of heavy-duty foil. Freeze for up to 2 weeks. Defrost on the countertop for several hours before cutting into bars.

"All you need is love. But a little chocolate now and then doesn't hurt."
CHARLES M. SCHULZ

Classic Pecan Bars

with Pat-in-the-Pan Crust

MAKES: 36 bars
BAKE TIME:
About 55 minutes
FREEZE ME!

People who regularly make brownies because they love the ease of one-bowl baking sometimes avoid recipes like this one, thinking that making a crust and then a topping is one step too many. But just take a look at the directions to see how simple the process is: The crust is actually just a mixture of loose, buttery crumbs that you press into the pan. The topping is simply a short list of ingredients whisked together and poured on top. The resulting bars have it all: A decadent, crumbly crust that supports a rich, gooey, sweet-but-not-too-sweet pecan pie–like topping.

FOR THE CRUST

2 cups unbleached all-purpose flour

⅔ cup confectioners' sugar

¼ cup cornstarch

2 teaspoons salt

14 tablespoons (1¾ sticks) unsalted butter, chilled and cut into 12 pieces

FOR THE FILLING

8 tablespoons (1 stick) unsalted butter, melted and cooled

1 cup packed light brown sugar

⅔ cup light corn syrup

2 large eggs

1 tablespoon pure vanilla extract

1 teaspoon salt

4 cups pecans, coarsely chopped

1. Preheat the oven to 350°F. Line a 9-by-13-inch baking pan with heavy-duty aluminum foil, making sure that the foil is tucked into all the corners and that there is at least 1 inch overhanging the top of the pan on all sides.

2. Make the crust: Place the flour, confectioners' sugar, cornstarch, and salt in a medium bowl and beat together with an electric mixer on low until combined. Add the butter and beat on low until the ingredients just begin to come together in clumps.

3. Sprinkle the crust mixture across the bottom of the prepared pan and press it into an even layer with your fingertips. Place the crust in the freezer, uncovered, until it firms up, about 15 minutes.

4. Bake the crust until the edges are just golden, 18 to 20 minutes. Remove

>> **A STEP AHEAD**

Remove the cooled, uncut bars from the pan by grasping the overhanging foil and pulling it up. Peel away the foil and wrap the bars in a double layer of plastic and then a layer of heavy-duty foil. Freeze for up to 2 weeks. Defrost on the countertop for several hours before cutting into bars.

Gobble, Gobble // PRE-THANKSGIVING COOKIE SWAP

I f you think about it, the first Thanksgiving wasn't that different from a cookie swap. The pilgrims, all shiny buckles and big hats, met up with their Wampanoag neighbors to swap and share their best food. Why not commemorate the event—and make the holidays easier on *your* neighbors, who are stressed about hosting their own feasts—by putting together a rapid-fire pre-Thanksgiving swap. Have everyone over a few days before Turkey Day, and suggest each person bring cookies appropriate for the holiday. Classic Pecan Bars with Pat-in-the-Pan Crust, Pumpkin Cheesecake Brownies (page 59), and Cranberry-Orange Shortbread Bars (see the variation on page 74) would all be good choices. Garnish your spread with maize or cute baby squash. Hand out turkey-shaped stress balls (available online) or pilgrim hats (see Party City in Resources, page 218) as party favors. Then dispatch your crowd early to get cracking on those casseroles!

the pan from the oven and reduce the oven temperature to 325°F.

5. Prepare the filling: Whisk together the butter, sugar, corn syrup, eggs, vanilla, and salt in a large bowl. Stir in the pecans.

6. Pour the filling over the hot crust and return the pan to the oven. Bake until the filling is just set, 30 to 35 minutes. Transfer the pan to a wire rack and let it cool completely. (The bars can be frozen at this point; see "A Step Ahead," page 71.)

7. Grasping the overhanging foil on either side of the pan, lift out the bars and place them on a cutting board. Use a sharp chef's knife to cut them into 36 bars; peel them from the foil.

Classic Pecan Bars with Pat-in-the-Pan Crust will keep in an airtight container at room temperature for 2 to 3 days.

"Cookies are made of butter and love."

NORWEGIAN PROVERB

Cherry-Almond Shortbread Bars

A cheery choice for a tea party or springtime swap.

I love a crumb bar recipe that uses the same mixture for the crust and the topping—even though the bars look like they took all day to make, preparation is really a snap. These are rich and buttery, with a great balance of sweet and tart. Using dried cherries in addition to preserves makes these bars deliciously chewy, and the flavors of cherries and almonds pair up dreamily.

MAKES: 36 bars
BAKE TIME:
25 to 30 minutes
QUICK PREP
FREEZE ME!

1 cup whole almonds

1 cup sugar

1 cup unbleached all-purpose flour

½ teaspoon salt

½ cup (1 stick) unsalted butter, chilled and cut into 8 pieces

½ teaspoon pure vanilla extract

1¼ cups cherry preserves

1 cup dried cherries (see Note)

1. Preheat the oven to 375°F. Line a 9-by-13-inch baking pan with heavy-duty aluminum foil, making sure that the foil is tucked into all the corners and that there is at least 1 inch overhanging the top of the pan on all sides.

2. Place the almonds and sugar in a food processor and pulse about 10 times until the nuts are finely

ground (the mixture should look like very coarse sand). Add the flour, salt, butter, and vanilla, and pulse another 8 to 10 times until the mixture is crumbly.

3. Transfer half of the almond mixture to the prepared pan and press it into a compact, even layer with your fingertips. Spread the preserves evenly over the dough with a rubber spatula. Sprinkle the dried cherries over this. Press the remaining almond mixture into loose, large crumbles and scatter them evenly over the cherries and preserves.

4. Bake until the jam is bubbling and the topping is golden, 25 to 30 minutes. Transfer the pan to a wire rack and let it cool completely. (The bars can be frozen at this point; see "A Step Ahead," left.)

5. Grasping the overhanging foil on either side of the pan, lift out the bars and place them on a cutting board. Cut into 36 pieces, and peel them from the foil.

Cherry-Almond Shortbread Bars will keep in an airtight container at room temperature for up to 3 days.

Note: Dried cherries are available in specialty foods stores and most supermarkets. Look for them near the raisins and dried apricots. If you can't find them locally, you can order them from King Arthur Flour (see Resources, page 216).

VARIATIONS

Other preserves and dried fruit combinations may be substituted for the cherry preserves and dried cherries, including apricot preserves and chopped, dried apricots; strawberry preserves and dried strawberries. You can also try mixing and matching: orange marmalade with dried cranberries, or peach preserves with golden raisins. Just avoid dried fruit that is too dry—apples, pears, pineapple, and mango will become unpleasantly tough when baked for this long.

THE BEST OF BOTH WORLDS

FLAKY PASTRY COOKIES

When cookies are called for but only the elegance of pastry will do, it's time to make swoon-worthy confections that borrow the best features of both. Made with pastry dough, and partaking of all that luxuriant layered goodness, these hybrids combine the buttery crumb of a tart with the diminutive cheerfulness of a cookie.

If you have a soft spot for tender cookies, choose a recipe that uses cream cheese dough. Cookies made with this type of dough—such as rugelach and pinwheels—are melt-in-your-mouth soft, and the tangy flavor of the cream cheese is a wonderful foil for their sweet and sticky fillings. This dough is extremely quick to make and a breeze to work with; it's also simple to assemble from items you probably have on hand.

If you are a fan of crisp and flaky baked goods, the recipes made with store-bought puff pastry are for you. It goes without saying that they're smart options for last-minute swap preparations. These cookies have layers of crunchy, crackly flakes that you will find irresistible. Brands made with vegetable shortening, such as Pepperidge Farm, will give you the flakiness but not the flavor of an all-butter brand like Dufour (my pastry of choice); both are available at many supermarkets and specialty food stores. If you have never used puff pastry before, try the Sacristans on page 83 first. The shaping of these cookies requires only the slightest effort: Roll out the dough, cut it into strips, and twist each strip a few times. That's it—and yet they look like you made a big fuss and got flour in your hair.

Both types of flaky pastry dough used in the following recipes freeze very well. In fact, the cookies keep their shape better and rise to a loftier height when the dough is well-chilled or even frozen. So as you'll see, I instruct you to freeze and chill the dough whenever appropriate. Follow all of these steps, however nitpicky they may seem, for best results.

Milk Chocolate and Cherry Rugelach

I've been making this rugelach dough for years, experimenting with fillings both classic (currants and walnuts) and creative (Heath English Toffee Bits, hazelnuts, and dark chocolate). Here is my current favorite, a combination of cherries, almonds, and milk chocolate. You'll notice that the yield on this recipe is slightly more than 3 dozen, because of the way the rolled dough is divided into 10 wedges. If you are baking by the dozens for your swap, you'll just have to keep a few extras for yourself!

MAKES: 40 rugelach
BAKE TIME:
20 to 25 minutes
FREEZE ME!

FOR THE DOUGH

2 cups unbleached all-purpose flour,
  plus extra for working the dough

1 tablespoon plus 1½ teaspoons sugar

¼ teaspoon salt

1 package (8 ounces) cream cheese,
  chilled and cut into pieces

1 cup (2 sticks) unsalted butter,
  chilled and cut into pieces

FOR THE FILLING AND FINISHING

½ cup sugar

1 teaspoon ground cinnamon

1 cup almonds

½ cup cherry preserves

6 ounces milk chocolate,
  finely chopped (about 1 cup)

⅔ cup dried cherries

¼ cup heavy cream

1. Make the dough: Place the flour, sugar, and salt in a food processor and pulse to combine. Add the cream cheese and butter and pulse until the mixture resembles coarse meal.

2. Turn the mixture out onto a lightly floured work surface and press it into a ball. Divide the ball into 4 equal pieces and shape each piece into a disk 4 inches in diameter. Wrap each disk in plastic and refrigerate for at least 3 hours (or up to 2 days). (The dough can be frozen at this point; see "A Step Ahead," opposite.)

3. Preheat the oven to 375°F. Line 2 baking sheets with parchment paper.

4. Make the filling: Combine the sugar and cinnamon in a small bowl. Place the almonds in a food processor and pulse 5 to 8 times until finely chopped (they should look like very coarse sand). Transfer the chopped almonds to a medium bowl. Place the preserves in the food processor (no need to clean the bowl after processing the nuts) and process until any large chunks are broken up. Transfer to a small bowl.

5. Remove one dough disk from the refrigerator and, with a lightly floured rolling pin on a lightly floured work surface, roll out the dough into a 9-inch round. Using a 9-inch plate

Party On

Cookies 'n' Candles // A HANUKKAH SWAP

Put the "festive" in "festival of lights" with a Hanukkah-themed cookie swap. Once you've chosen one of the eight nights of light, bake a batch or two of rugelach (or try the Chocolate-Walnut Mandelbrot on page 159), and ask your friends to bring over their favorite cookies. Cue up *Woody Guthrie's Happy Joyous Hanukkah* by the Klezmatics, *Hanukkah Rocks* by the Leevees, or *Hanukkah Swings* by Kenny Ellis. To entertain your friends before the swap begins, set out cups of crayons and cardboard menorahs (order a twelve-pack from www.oytoys.com), and have everyone color their own table decorations while they nibble on potato latkes. Dreidels and Hanukkah gelt can be had for very little *actual* gelt—and they can be used for party games and/or party favors.

or pie plate as a guide, trim the edges with a sharp paring knife to make a neat circle.

6. Spread 2 tablespoons plus 1½ teaspoons of the preserves over the dough. Sprinkle evenly with ⅓ cup of chocolate. Then sprinkle evenly with 5 tablespoons of the cherries. Sprinkle with 2 tablespoons of the cinnamon sugar. Sprinkle with 5 tablespoons of the almonds. Pat the filling firmly with your fingertips to secure it to the dough. Cut the dough circle into 10 wedges. Roll each wedge into a crescent, beginning at the wide edge and rolling toward the point, and place it on the prepared baking sheet, point facing down. Place the baking sheet in the freezer until firm and well chilled, 30 minutes to 1 hour.

7. Repeat steps 5 and 6 with the remaining dough disks. (The shaped cookies can be frozen at this point; see "A Step Ahead," right.)

8. Brush the chilled rugelach with the heavy cream and bake them until they are golden, 20 to 25 minutes. Transfer them to wire racks with a metal spatula and let them cool completely.

Milk Chocolate and Cherry Rugelach will keep in an airtight container at room temperature for 2 to 3 days.

VARIATION
Slice-and-Bake Rugelach

Making these cookies in a spiral shape is quicker than the standard recipe and yields 60 small cookies rather than 40 large ones. Although preparing the dough this way affects the size of the cookies, the end result is similar—they're still tender and delicious. Leave out the dried cherries, using just the preserves (the cherries are too bulky and will make rolling the dough into a cylinder difficult). Here's how to shape them:

1. Roll out the dough into two 6-inch squares, then wrap them in plastic and refrigerate for at least 2 hours (or up to 2 days). Roll each square out into a rough 10½-inch square, trimming the edges with a sharp paring knife so it is an even 10-inch square. Spread the preserves evenly over the dough squares, then sprinkle with the chocolate, cinnamon sugar, and nuts. Roll the dough squares into tight cylinders. Wrap the cylinders in plastic wrap and place them in the freezer for 1 hour to firm up. (The dough can

>> **A STEP AHEAD**

The rugelach dough can be frozen, wrapped in a double layer of plastic and a layer of heavy-duty foil, for up to 1 month; defrost it overnight in the refrigerator before using it to make cookies.

The shaped cookies can also be frozen on the baking sheets, transferred to ziplock bags, and stored in the freezer for up to 1 month. Transfer the frozen cookies to parchment-lined baking sheets, brush them with the cream, and bake for a minute or two longer than directed.

be wrapped in an additional layer of plastic and a layer of heavy-duty foil, and frozen for up to 2 weeks; defrost it in the refrigerator overnight before proceeding.)

2. Preheat the oven to 375°F. Line several baking sheets with parchment paper.

3. Slice the dough into ⅓-inch-thick rounds, rotating the dough often so it doesn't become misshapen as you cut. Arrange the cookies about an inch apart on the baking sheets.

4. Bake the rugelach spirals until golden brown, 15 to 20 minutes. Transfer the baking sheet to a wire rack and let the cookies cool completely on the sheet.

Slice-and-Bake Rugelach will keep in an airtight container at room temperature for 2 to 3 days.

SMART COOKIE

From Scraps to Splendid   LEFTOVER RUGELACH DOUGH

Instead of throwing away your dough scraps, think Pastry Dough Part II. To make yummy cinnamon spirals, gather the scraps into a ball and roll it into a ¼-inch-thick square. Sprinkle the top liberally with cinnamon sugar, and roll the dough around the filling into a tight cylinder (about 2 inches wide). Wrap the cylinder in plastic and refrigerate for up to 3 days (or freeze for up to 2 weeks). Then defrost the log in the refrigerator overnight, slice it into ⅓-inch-thick circles, place them on a parchment-lined sheet, and bake as directed in the Slice-and-Bake Rugelach variation above.

"Once in a young lifetime one should be allowed to have as much sweetness as one can possibly want and hold."

JUDITH OLNEY

Flaky Pastry Pinwheels

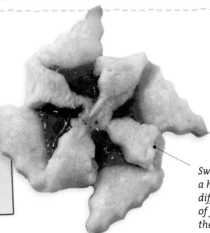

Swapping for a holiday? Use different colors of jam to suit the occasion.

Pinwheels are like cookie dough origami. The dough is fun to cut and fold, and the finished cookies are so pretty, it's like you put them in a box and toted them home from the bakery. Dusting the cookies with white sanding sugar always looks great, but you can coordinate the preserves with colored sanding sugar, if you like. Apricot preserves and orange sugar are festive for fall and Halloween, strawberry or raspberry preserves with pink sugar works well for Valentine's Day, and blueberry preserves with red and white sugar is just right for all-American holidays such as Memorial Day, Fourth of July, and Labor Day, or even Bastille Day, for our friends across the pond.

MAKES: 48 cookies
BAKE TIME: 12 to 15 minutes
FREEZE ME!

2 cup unbleached all-purpose flour,
plus extra for working the dough

½ cup sugar

½ teaspoon salt

1 package (8 ounces) cream cheese,
chilled and cut into 8 pieces

1 cup (2 sticks) unsalted butter,
chilled and cut into 16 pieces

⅓ cup raspberry or strawberry
preserves (seedless or seeded,
whichever you prefer)

1 large egg, lightly beaten

¼ cup coarse sanding sugar
(optional; see Resources, page 216)

1. Line several baking sheets with parchment paper.

2. Place the flour, sugar, and salt in a food processor and pulse to combine. Add the cream cheese and butter and pulse until the ingredients are just

≫ A STEP AHEAD

Shaped pinwheels can be frozen on the baking sheets for 1 hour, then transferred to a ziplock freezer bag, and stored in the freezer for up to 2 weeks. Transfer the frozen pinwheels to parchment-lined baking sheets and bake as directed.

combined and the mixture resembles coarse meal (do not overprocess).

3. Turn the mixture out onto a lightly floured work surface and shape the dough into two 6-inch squares. Wrap the dough squares in plastic and refrigerate them for at least 2 hours (or up to 2 days).

4. Remove one of the dough squares from the refrigerator and, with a lightly floured rolling pin on a lightly floured surface, roll it out into a rough 12½-by-8½-inch rectangle. Trim the edges with a fluted pastry wheel so it measures exactly 12 by 8 inches.

5. Use the fluted pastry wheel to cut the dough into 2-inch squares. Place the squares 1 inch apart on the prepared baking sheets, and store in the refrigerator.

6. Repeat Steps 4 and 5 with the remaining dough.

7. Preheat the oven to 375°F.

8. Use the fluted pastry wheel to cut ¾-inch diagonal slits from the corners of each square toward the center (as if you were cutting an **X** in the dough—but don't cut through the center!). Place ¼ teaspoon of preserves in the center of each square. With the tip of a knife, lift every other point and fold it into the center, overlapping the points of the folded tips slightly over the preserves. Repeat with the remaining squares. (The dough can be frozen at this point; see "A Step Ahead," left.)

9. Lightly brush the cookies with the beaten egg and sprinkle liberally with the sanding sugar if you wish. Bake until the edges of the cookies are deeply golden, 12 to 15 minutes. Transfer the baking sheets to wire racks and let the cookies cool completely.

Flaky Pastry Pinwheels will keep, layered between parchment paper, in an airtight container at room temperature for 2 to 3 days.

Pistachio Sacristans

Crisp, elegant, and ideal for a bridal shower swap.

The trick to working with puff pastry is to keep it as cold as possible at all times: While you are rolling it, while you are coating it with nuts and sugar, while you are cutting it, and while you are twisting it. Don't forget to chill the pastry twists well before baking them. This will help them keep their shape in the oven.

MAKES: 48 cookies
BAKE TIME: 15 minutes
QUICK PREP
FREEZE ME!

Unbleached all-purpose flour, for rolling the pastry

2 sheets (about 8 ounces each) frozen puff pastry, thawed but still chilled (see page 85)

1 cup turbinado sugar (Sugar in the Raw)

1 cup finely chopped pistachio nuts

1 large egg

1. Line 2 baking sheets with parchment paper. With a lightly floured rolling pin on a lightly floured surface, roll out one of the puff pastry sheets into a 12-inch square. Carefully slide the pastry onto a baking sheet, cover it with plastic wrap, and refrigerate it for 30 minutes. Repeat with the remaining puff pastry sheet.

2. Combine the sugar and nuts in a medium bowl. In a small bowl, whisk together the egg and 2 tablespoons of water.

3. Remove one of the pastry sheets from the refrigerator. Brush the top with a quarter of the egg mixture and sprinkle with a quarter of the sugar mixture. Pat the pastry with your fingertips to make sure that the sugar

›› A STEP AHEAD

Shaped sacristans can be frozen on the baking sheets for 1 hour, then transferred to a ziplock freezer bag and stored in the freezer for up to 2 weeks. Transfer the frozen sacristans to parchment-lined baking sheets and bake as directed.

Waste Not, Want Not

PUFF PASTRY LEFTOVERS

Don't put your pastry scraps out to pasture— there's life in them yet. Collect any leftover puff pastry in a ziplock bag in the freezer. When you have more than 8 ounces, defrost the scraps in the refrigerator, press them into a ball, and roll the ball into a ¼-inch-thick sheet. Cut the sheet with a small, fluted pastry cutter or a small heart-shaped cookie cutter. Place the pieces on a parchment-lined baking sheet, brush them with beaten egg, and sprinkle liberally with cinnamon sugar or Parmesan cheese. Bake in a 400°F oven until golden brown, 9 to 12 minutes.

and nuts adhere to it. Gently flip the pastry over, brush it with another quarter of the egg wash, and sprinkle it with another quarter of the sugar mixture.

4. Use a pastry wheel to cut the pastry sheet in half to form two 12-by-6-inch rectangles. Cut each rectangle into twelve 1-inch-wide strips. Gently twist each strip 4 times and place on the parchment-lined baking sheets at least 1½ inches apart from each other. Place in the freezer for 15 minutes. (The shaped cookies can be frozen at this point, see "A Step Ahead," page 83.)

5. Meanwhile, preheat the oven to 375°F.

6. Bake the cookies until they are puffed and golden, about 15 minutes.

Cool the baked cookies completely on the baking sheets.

7. Repeat with the remaining puff pastry sheet.

Pistachio Sacristans will keep in an airtight container at room temperature for up to 3 days.

VARIATION

Pumpkin Seed Sacristans

Unsalted pumpkin seeds (*pepitas*) give sacristans a beautiful color and wonderful aroma when baked. To make Pumpkin Seed Sacristans— a marvelously crunchy variation— substitute 1 cup of finely chopped unsalted pepitas for the pistachios, and use regular granulated sugar mixed with ½ teaspoon ground cinnamon instead of the turbinado sugar.

SMART COOKIE

Stay Puf't WORKING WITH PUFF PASTRY

Frozen puff pastry is one of the world's most delicious convenience foods. To get the most out of it, consider the following:

✳ Puff pastry handles best and puffs up highest at the right temperature: chilled but not frozen. It thaws very quickly—in about 15 minutes—on the countertop, or you can defrost it in the refrigerator for several hours or overnight (let it sit on the countertop for 5 minutes before rolling it). Before you begin to roll it out, make sure that it's cold but not still frozen, since frozen puff pastry will crack and break instead of rolling out smoothly. If it gets very soft as you work with it, put it back in the freezer for 5 minutes to firm up.

✳ Use a very sharp knife or pastry wheel to cut the pastry. A dull knife will compress the layers of dough, resulting in a low rise.

✳ Refrigerate or freeze your cut puff pastry before baking. It will rise and keep its shape better if it is cold when it goes into the oven.

✳ Make sure to bake your puff pastry adequately. You want it to be crisp throughout, which means the exterior should be a deep golden brown. If you let it bake just until it is light golden, the interior will be doughy and moist.

"Work is the meat of life, pleasure the dessert."

B. C. FORBES

Cardamom Palmiers

A **little bit of cardamom and ginger** added to the cinnamon sugar typically found on palmiers, or elephant ears, gives these miniature cookies an out-of-the-ordinary, slightly lemony flavor.

½ cup sugar, plus more for sprinkling
the work surface

½ teaspoon ground cardamom

¼ teaspoon ground cinnamon

¼ teaspoon ground ginger

1 sheet (about 8 ounces) frozen puff
pastry, thawed but well chilled

Flour, for dusting the rolling pin

1 large egg, lightly beaten

1. Combine ½ cup sugar and the cardamom, cinnamon, and ginger in a small bowl.

2. Dust the work surface with a tablespoon or two of sugar. Place the puff pastry on the work surface and quickly roll it with a lightly floured rolling pin into a 12-by-9-inch rectangle.

3. Brush the puff pastry with the beaten egg. Sprinkle the spiced sugar mixture over the pastry, patting it lightly with your fingers so that it adheres.

4. With the tip of a paring knife, mark a line lengthwise down the center of the pastry (do not cut through!).

Carefully roll each of the long sides of the rectangle toward the center line, leaving ⅓ inch uncovered on either side of the center line. Wrap the rolled pastry in plastic and refrigerate until firm, at least 2 hours and up to 2 days. (The pastry dough can be frozen at this point; see "A Step Ahead," right.)

5. Preheat the oven to 375°F. Line several baking sheets with parchment paper.

6. Use a sharp knife or pastry wheel to cut the pastry roll into ¼-inch slices. Arrange the slices 1 inch apart on the baking sheets.

7. Bake the cookies until golden brown, 15 to 20 minutes. Cool on the baking sheets for 15 to 20 minutes and then carefully slide the parchment paper with the cookies to a wire rack to cool completely.

Cardamom Palmiers will keep in an airtight container at room temperature for up to 3 days.

VARIATION
Savory Palmiers

Savory Palmiers are wonderful with cocktails and easy to make. Omit the sugar and substitute a thin layer of basil pesto, olive tapenade, or pureed sun-dried tomatoes and grated Parmesan (a few tablespoons should do) for the cardamom sugar filling. Proceed as directed.

>> **A STEP AHEAD**
The puff pastry roll can be wrapped in a double layer of plastic and then in a layer of heavy-duty foil and frozen for up to 2 weeks. Defrost it overnight in the refrigerator before proceeding as directed.

Sweet Charity // COOKIE SWAPPING FOR A CAUSE

Bake a cookie, change the world. Cookie swaps seem ready-made for fund-raising and other do-gooder activities. Cookies are the ambassadors of the dessert world—they cross all party lines and appeal to people of all ages and persuasions. Here are a few ways to spread the love, one cookie at a time:

✳ **Extra, Extra!** Ask everyone to bring an extra dozen cookies (simply bake up a portion of extra dough, and freeze the rest for later). During the swap, package these extras for a local senior center or hospice, and deliver them right after the party.

✳ **Can It** Ask guests to bring canned goods or other nonperishable items along with cookies, and bring these donations to your local food bank.

✳ **A Run for Your Money** Plan your cookie exchange as an after-party for a 5K charitable walk or run. See how much money you and your friends can raise for a good cause, and celebrate your success with cookies. (And hey, there's no guilt—you just burned off all those calories!)

✳ **Swap and Deliver** Get a U-Haul or borrow your neighbor's minivan. Ask people to bring bags of old clothes and other gently used donate-able items, and after cookie-swapping, drive them all to Goodwill or a charitable thrift store to give them away. It will help clean out your closets and do a service to your community at the same time.

Chapter 6

REFRIGERATOR MADNESS

INSANELY GOOD ICEBOX COOKIES

As a cooking school intern at a four-star Manhattan kitchen, I learned a lot of useful things: how to pit a mango, what to do with leftover egg whites after making custard for one hundred, why working with phyllo dough is always a race against time (and occasionally the reason for a crying jag). But the most eye-opening lesson came from watching the pastry chef use his refrigerator and freezer just as much as his oven to produce incredible desserts. With cold storage, it was possible to effortlessly produce amazing items in a short amount of time. Turns out, home bakers can do the same.

To make icebox cookies—which can be flavored with everything from anise to vanilla and studded with chips, nuts, and more—you prepare the dough up to a month in advance, shape it into logs, and refrigerate or freeze it until you need it (I give you specific instructions on how to do this in each recipe). On the day of your party, you need only turn on the oven, let the dough soften slightly on the countertop, slice it, and bake it.

To shape even, smooth logs, place roughly shaped dough on a piece of wax or parchment paper and roll the dough inside the paper on the countertop. Then peel the paper away before wrapping the dough tightly in a double layer of plastic wrap and a layer of heavy-duty aluminum foil and chilling it. If your dough is very soft, one side may flatten slightly in the fridge. So once the dough firms up a little, roll the log back and forth on the countertop a few times to restore its shape before placing it back in the fridge.

Chilled dough should be softened slightly before you cut into it—if it is hard, it may crumble or shatter. Defrost frozen dough in the refrigerator overnight or on the countertop for a few hours, and let refrigerated dough soften for a few minutes on the countertop (if it it gets too soft, pop it in the freezer for 10 to 15 minutes to firm up). When slicing, rotate the log often so one side doesn't become flattened by the knife.

And remember, there is no law mandating that icebox cookies be round. It is possible to shape dough into squared-off or rectangular logs. Edging your cookies with colored sugar or chopped nuts can make them beautiful, as can pressing chocolate-covered espresso beans or M&M's onto the tops. Go ahead, gild the lily.

Vanilla Icebox Cookies

These versatile cookies love to play dress up— here they're dipped in chocolate and sprinkled with nonpareils.

A cookie for all occasions if ever there was one, this icebox cookie has irresistible vanilla fragrance and flavor and is wonderfully versatile. For a kid-friendly cookie party, try brushing the logs of dough with egg whites and rolling them in multicolored sprinkles before slicing and baking. To get a chocolate-and-vanilla combo, dip half of each baked cookie in some melted bittersweet or milk chocolate, placing the dipped cookies on a parchment-lined baking sheet, and refrigerate them for 5 minutes to allow the chocolate to set up. Play around with the decorations—this cookie is an ideal (and delicious) canvas.

MAKES: 48 cookies
BAKE TIME:
13 to 15 minutes
QUICK PREP
FREEZE ME!

2 cups unbleached all-purpose flour

½ teaspoon baking powder

½ teaspoon salt

1 cup (2 sticks) unsalted butter, at room temperature

¾ cup sugar

1 large egg

2 teaspoons pure vanilla extract

1. Combine the flour, baking powder, and salt in a medium bowl.

2. Place the butter and sugar in a large bowl and beat together with an electric mixer on medium-high until fluffy, 2 to 3 minutes. Add the egg and vanilla and beat until smooth. Beat in the flour mixture on low until just incorporated.

>> A STEP AHEAD

Dough logs can be wrapped in a double layer of plastic and then in a layer of heavy-duty foil and frozen for up to 1 month. Defrost the dough in the refrigerator for at least 5 hours or overnight before proceeding as directed.

3. Divide the dough in half. Turn one portion out onto a piece of wax paper and shape it, rolling it inside the paper, into a log about 8 inches long. Wrap the dough in plastic and refrigerate it for at least 2 hours (or up to 24 hours). Repeat with the remaining dough. (The dough can be frozen at this point; see "A Step Ahead," left.)

4. Remove the dough from the refrigerator and let it stand on the countertop until softened slightly, about 15 minutes. Meanwhile, preheat the oven to 350°F.

5. Using a sharp knife, slice the dough into ⅓-inch-thick rounds, rotating the dough often so it doesn't become misshapen as you cut. Place the cookies at least 2 inches apart on ungreased baking sheets.

6. Bake the cookies until they are lightly golden around the edges but still soft on top, 13 to 15 minutes. Let them stand on the baking sheet for 5 minutes and then remove them with a metal spatula to a wire rack to cool completely.

Vanilla Icebox Cookies will keep in an airtight container at room temperature for 3 to 4 days.

VARIATIONS

Chocolate Slice-and-Bakes

Reduce the flour to 1½ cups and add ½ cup of unsweetened Dutch-process cocoa to the flour mixture. Brush the dough logs with beaten egg white and roll them in chocolate sprinkles before slicing and baking.

Chocolate Chip Slice-and-Bakes

This is a lighter, more crumbly, and less chewy chocolate chip cookie than your standard drop version, with a sandy, shortbread-like texture. Use 6 tablespoons of granulated sugar and 6 tablespoons of packed light brown sugar. Stir 1 cup of mini chocolate chips into the dough before shaping it into logs.

Lime and Coconut Slice-and-Bakes

Add 1½ teaspoons grated lime zest to the butter and sugar during Step 2. Add

½ teaspoon of pure coconut extract to the dough along with the vanilla. Stir 1 cup of sweetened flaked coconut into the dough before shaping the logs. Brush the logs with beaten egg white and roll them in chopped unsalted cashews or macadamia nuts before slicing and baking.

Cranberry-Orange Slice-and-Bakes

Add 2 teaspoons of grated orange zest to the butter and sugar during Step 2. Add 1 cup of chopped dried cranberries to the dough before shaping into logs. Brush the logs with beaten egg white and roll them in sugar mixed with a little ground cardamom before slicing and baking.

WHERE THE BOYS ARE   REAL MEN SWAP COOKIES

There's some evidence that men are taking a growing interest in cookie swaps. More than ten years ago, a group of male teachers at Arbor Heights Elementary School in Seattle were so sick of being left out of an annual ladies' exchange, they decided to throw one for themselves. Since then, they've made it an annual male-bonding event. They have a website, menbakebetter.com, with tips, recipes, and links to other dudes-only exchanges in the Pacific Northwest. They suggest using tongue-in-cheek humor to convince men to bake cookies (in their invitation, they declare they will "cream some butter with our bare hands" and "beat some eggs within an inch of their lives"). They even have a theme song, "Bakin', bakin', bakin' / All the cookies makin' . . . ," sung to the tune of "Rawhide."

If half (or all) of your guests are men, consider them when buying party favors. Instead of cookie-scented lip gloss, for example, give out instant-read thermometers from Sur La Table (www.surlatable.com) in Day-Glo colors. Guys love gadgets.

Control Your Temper   HOW TO MELT CHOCOLATE

It's easy—and tasty—to embellish cookies by dipping them in chocolate. But if you want your chocolate to have a shiny, professional-looking finish, you have to handle it properly when you are melting it; otherwise it will separate and become grainy in the process. Melting the chocolate so it remains smooth and rehardens to resemble the shiny, snappy bar or block it once was is called "tempering."

Now, you may have heard of tempering . . . it's a fairly painstaking process in which chocolate must be heated to precisely 105 degrees, and then brought back down to and maintained at a temperature of 88 degrees. If allowed to drop below 88 degrees too quickly, the cocoa butter molecules in the chocolate link up loosely, making the chocolate dull and soft when it finally returns to room temperature.

Tempering may sound like a pain—and that's because it is! But don't despair: If you're working with just a small amount (well under a pound) of chocolate needed to decorate cookies, you can skip tempering altogether. Simply take care to melt your chocolate in such a way that it doesn't go *out* of temper (meaning that the majority of the cocoa butter in the chocolate maintains its tight crystal structure),

and you won't have to worry about getting it back *into* temper. Here's how:

❋ **In the microwave:** Finely chop your chocolate and place two-thirds of it in a microwave-safe bowl. Microwave for 30 seconds on high, then remove it, and check it. If there are still chunks of hard chocolate in the bowl, microwave again for another 30 seconds. If the chocolate has softened all the way through but still maintains its chopped chocolate appearance (it shouldn't be runny or liquid at this point, just very, very soft), add the remaining one-third of the chocolate and whisk until smooth. The solid chocolate will have enough cocoa butter crystals to encourage the formation of these crystals in the melted chocolate, so the chocolate will set up nice and shiny when it cools.

❋ **On the stovetop:** Finely chop your chocolate and place two-thirds of it in the top of a double boiler or a bowl set over a pot of barely simmering water. Let the chocolate stand, stirring it occasionally, until it is just melted, but no longer. Remove the bowl from the heat and whisk in the remaining chocolate. You'll get the same tempered result as with the microwave by adding a substantial amount of in-temper chocolate to the melted chocolate.

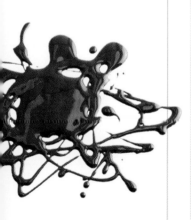

Biscochito Icebox Cookies

Officially adopted by New Mexico as its state cookie, tender and tasty biscochitos are also baked in large swaths of Texas and all over Mexico. Rolled and cut into diamond shapes, they are often served at weddings as a symbol of purity. I love the traditional Mexican flavor combination of anise and cinnamon in cookies of every shape, but especially in these thin, crispy-chewy slice-and-bake rounds.

MAKES: 48 cookies
BAKE TIME:
12 to 14 minutes
QUICK PREP
FREEZE ME!

¾ **cup granulated sugar**

½ **teaspoon ground cinnamon**

2¼ **cups unbleached all-purpose flour**

½ **teaspoon baking powder**

¼ **teaspoon salt**

2 **teaspoons anise seeds,**
   finely ground in a coffee grinder
   (¾ teaspoon ground)

1 **cup (2 sticks) unsalted butter,**
   at room temperature

½ **cup packed light brown sugar**

2 **large eggs**

1 **teaspoon pure vanilla extract**

2 **teaspoons brandy**

1. Combine ¼ cup granulated sugar and the ground cinnamon in a small bowl. Set aside.

2. Combine the flour, baking powder, salt, and anise in a medium bowl.

>> A STEP AHEAD

A STEP AHEAD

Dough logs can be wrapped in a double layer of plastic and then a layer of heavy-duty foil and frozen for up to 1 month. Defrost the dough in the refrigerator for at least 5 hours or overnight before proceeding as directed from Step 5.

3. Place the butter, remaining granulated sugar, and brown sugar in a large bowl and beat together with an electric mixer on medium-high until fluffy, 2 to 3 minutes. Add the eggs, vanilla, and brandy and beat until smooth. Beat in the flour mixture on low until just incorporated.

4. Divide the dough in half. Turn one portion out onto a piece of wax paper and shape it, rolling it inside the paper, into an 8-inch-long log. Wrap the dough in plastic and refrigerate it for at least 2 hours (or for up to 24 hours). Repeat with the remaining dough. (The dough can be frozen at this point; see "A Step Ahead," left.)

5. Remove the dough from the refrigerator and let it stand on the countertop until softened slightly, about 15 minutes.

6. Meanwhile, preheat the oven to 350°F. Line several baking sheets with parchment paper.

7. Slice the dough into ⅓-inch-thick rounds and place the rounds at least 2 inches apart on the baking sheets. Brush the tops with some water (about 1 tablespoon total) and sprinkle them generously with the cinnamon sugar.

8. Bake the cookies until they are lightly golden around the edges but still soft on top, 12 to 14 minutes. Let them stand on the baking sheet for 5 minutes and then carefully slide the parchment paper with the cookies to a wire rack to cool completely.

Biscochito Icebox Cookies will keep in an airtight container at room temperature for 2 to 3 days.

YES WE CAN :: LOBBYING FOR YOUR STATE COOKIE

New Mexico isn't the only state with its own cookie. In Massachusetts (birthplace of the Toll House cookie), legislators have given the chocolate chipper state-cookie status. But other states have been slow to follow suit.

Even New York, which has a state muffin (the apple muffin), and Florida, which has a state beverage (orange juice), have not jumped on the bandwagon. If your state doesn't have a cookie, write to your legislator. Make a difference today!

Viva Galletas! // A CINCO DE MAYO SWAP

Celebrate this day of Mexican culture and pride with a cookie swap? *Por qué no?* Simply pull together sweets, snacks, and decorations that evoke our sunny neighbor to the south. Get the fiesta started with Biscochito Icebox Cookies, and, if your guests are looking for suggestions, recommend Maple-Walnut Wedding Cakes (page 129; a twist on traditional Mexican wedding cakes), Chocolate-Caramel Graham Cracker Sandwiches (page 193; let's call them Dulce de Leche Sandwich Cookies for today), and Pumpkin Seed Sacristans (page 84). Mexican and southwestern appetizers such as guacamole, quesadillas, and albondigas (Mexican meatballs) are festive and easy to prepare. To drink? How about Mexican beer, such as Tecate or Negra Modelo, and Jarritos Mexican sodas in tropical fruit flavors like tamarind, mango, and guayaba (guava)? Pitchers of Fresh Lime Margaritas (page 213) will also help get the party going. Spruce up your swap table with tissue-paper flowers, and use a colorful piñata as a centerpiece. Fill goody bags with loot from Mexgrocer.com—I like to give and get small bags of dried chile peppers, bottles of hot sauce, and Mexican candy. You can order a variety of beautiful and incredibly inexpensive mesh and oilcloth bags to pack away these goodies from Directfrommexico.com, where rolls of oilcloth can also be purchased to be used, and reused, as table coverings.

Gingery Chocolate-Orange Slice-and-Bakes

Crystallized ginger adds a touch of heat to these flavorful cookies.

MAKES: 48 cookies
BAKE TIME:
13 to 15 minutes
QUICK PREP
FREEZE ME!

Candied orange peel and crystallized ginger give these chocolate chip icebox cookies great fruit-and-spice flavor. You can shape the dough into regular logs to make round cookies, but I love the elegant shape of thin rectangles.

2 cups unbleached all-purpose flour

½ teaspoon baking powder

¼ teaspoon salt

10 tablespoons unsalted butter, at room temperature

½ cup granulated sugar

¼ cup packed light brown sugar

2 large eggs

1 teaspoon pure vanilla extract

1 cup mini semisweet chocolate chips

½ cup candied orange peel, finely chopped (see Notes)

2 tablespoons finely chopped crystallized ginger (see Notes)

1. Combine the flour, baking powder, and salt in a medium mixing bowl.

2. Combine the butter and sugars in a large mixing bowl and beat together with an electric mixer on

medium-high speed until fluffy, 2 to 3 minutes. Add the eggs and vanilla and beat until smooth. Stir in the flour mixture until just incorporated. Stir in the chocolate chips, orange peel, and ginger.

3. Divide the dough in half. Turn one portion onto a piece of wax paper and shape it, patting it inside the paper, into a rectangular log about 8 inches long, 1 inch high, and 2 inches wide. Wrap the dough in plastic and refrigerate it for at least 2 hours (or for up to 24 hours). Repeat with the remaining dough. (The dough can be frozen at this point; see "A Step Ahead," right.)

4. Remove the dough from the refrigerator and let it stand on the countertop until softened slightly, about 15 minutes. Meanwhile, preheat the oven to 350°F.

5. Slice the dough into ⅓-inch-thick rectangles, rotating the dough often so it doesn't become misshapen as you cut. Place the cookies at least 2 inches apart on ungreased baking sheets.

6. Bake the cookies until they are lightly golden around the edges but still soft on top, 13 to 15 minutes. Let them stand on the baking sheet for 5 minutes and then remove them with a metal spatula to a wire rack to cool completely.

Gingery Chocolate-Orange Slice-and-Bakes will keep in an airtight container at room temperature for 3 to 4 days.

Notes: Candied orange peel can be found in the baking aisle at the supermarket, near the sprinkles, candied cherries, and other baking garnishes. Crystallized ginger, also called candied ginger, can be found at most gourmet food shops and in the spice aisle at some supermarkets.

>> **A STEP AHEAD**
Dough logs can be wrapped in a double layer of plastic and then a layer of heavy-duty foil and frozen for up to 1 month. Defrost the dough in the refrigerator for at least 5 hours or overnight before proceeding as directed from Step 4.

Espresso Squares

Like a cup of dark coffee in cookie form.

These sophisticated squares make the perfect after-dinner sweet. Their powerful espresso flavor satisfies like a cup of strong coffee. I like to press a chocolate-covered espresso bean into each one before baking, but for a sweeter touch you could press some Heath English Toffee Bits into the tops instead, or drizzle melted chocolate over each cooled cookie.

MAKES: 48 cookies
BAKE TIME: 13 to 14 minutes
QUICK PREP
FREEZE ME!

1 tablespoon instant espresso powder

1 tablespoon boiling water

2 cups unbleached all-purpose flour

½ teaspoon baking powder

¼ teaspoon salt

10 tablespoons unsalted butter, at room temperature

⅔ cup light brown sugar

2 large eggs

1 teaspoon pure vanilla extract

48 chocolate-covered espresso beans (optional)

1. Stir together the espresso powder and boiling water in a cup. Set aside to cool.

2. Combine the flour, baking powder, and salt in a medium bowl.

3. Place the butter and sugar in a large bowl and beat together with an electric mixer on medium-high until fluffy, 2 to 3 minutes. Add the eggs, vanilla, and espresso mixture and beat until smooth. Beat in the flour mixture on low until just incorporated.

4. Divide the dough in half. Turn one portion out onto a piece of wax paper and shape it, rolling it inside the paper and pressing it flat on four sides, into a squared-off log about 8 inches long. Wrap the dough in plastic and freeze it for 2 hours. Repeat with the remaining dough. (The dough can be frozen for a longer period; see "A Step Ahead," right.)

5. Place the dough on the countertop and let it stand until softened slightly, about 15 minutes. Meanwhile, preheat the oven to 350°F.

6. Slice the dough into ⅓-inch-thick squares, rotating the dough often so it doesn't become misshapen as you cut. Place the cookies at least 2 inches apart on ungreased baking sheets.

7. Bake the cookies for 10 minutes (they'll still be moist) and then remove from the oven and carefully press an espresso bean, if desired, into the center of each cookie. Continue to bake until they are lightly golden around the edges and just dry on top, 3 to 4 minutes more. Let them stand on the baking sheet for 5 minutes and then remove them with a metal spatula to a wire rack to cool completely.

Espresso Squares will keep in an airtight container at room temperature for 3 to 4 days.

VARIATIONS

Mocha Squares

Reduce the flour to 1¾ cups and add ¼ cup of sifted unsweetened Dutch-process cocoa powder to the dry ingredients in Step 2.

Coffee–Chocolate Chip Squares

Add 1 cup of mini chocolate chips to the dough after the flour mixture is incorporated in Step 3.

>> **A STEP AHEAD**

Dough logs can be wrapped in a double layer of plastic and then a layer of heavy-duty foil and frozen for up to 1 month. Defrost the dough in the refrigerator for at least 5 hours or overnight before proceeding as directed from Step 5.

Lemon–Poppy Seed Cornmeal Cookies

MAKES: 48 cookies
BAKE TIME:
12 to 15 minutes
QUICK PREP
FREEZE ME!

The name of this cookie is a mouthful, which is appropriate for a treat that's got so much flavor (like your favorite lemon–poppy seed muffin) and texture (a bit crunchy from the cornmeal and poppy seeds). I love the elegance and subtle nuttiness of the poppy seed coating, but you could substitute a brightly colored sanding sugar—turquoise is a showstopper, as is hot pink—if you prefer.

1½ cups unbleached all-purpose flour

⅔ cup yellow cornmeal

¼ teaspoon salt

¾ cup (1½ sticks) unsalted butter,
    at room temperature

⅔ cup sugar

2 teaspoons lemon zest

2 large eggs

1 teaspoon pure vanilla extract

½ cup poppy seeds

1 large egg white

1. Combine the flour, cornmeal, and salt in a medium bowl.

2. Place the butter, sugar, and lemon zest in a large bowl and beat together

with an electric mixer on medium until fluffy, about 3 minutes. Add the eggs and vanilla and beat until smooth. Beat in the flour mixture on low until just combined.

3. Divide the dough in half. Turn one portion out onto a piece of wax paper and shape it, rolling it inside the paper, into an 8-inch-long cylinder. Wrap it in plastic and freeze it for 2 hours. Repeat with the remaining dough. (The dough can be frozen for a longer period; see "A Step Ahead," right.)

4. Place the dough on the countertop and let it stand until softened slightly, about 15 minutes. Meanwhile, preheat the oven to 350°F.

5. Spread the poppy seeds on a rimmed baking sheet. Brush each dough log with beaten egg white and roll it in the poppy seeds to coat. Slice the dough into ⅓-inch-thick rounds, rotating the dough often so it doesn't become misshapen as you cut. Place the cookies at least 2 inches apart on ungreased baking sheets.

6. Bake the cookies until they're set and lightly colored around the edges, 12 to 15 minutes. Let them stand on the baking sheets for 5 minutes and then remove them with a metal spatula to a wire rack to cool completely.

Lemon–Poppy Seed Cornmeal Cookies will keep in an airtight container at room temperature for 3 to 4 days.

>> **A STEP AHEAD**
Dough logs can be wrapped in a double layer of plastic and then a layer of heavy-duty foil and frozen for up to 1 month. Defrost the dough in the refrigerator for at least 5 hours or overnight before proceeding as directed from Step 4.

Chocolate-Pistachio Spiral Cookies

Kids love the lollipop-like swirl of these tender cookies.

MAKES: 48 cookies
BAKE TIME: 12 minutes
FREEZE ME!

Rolling together pistachio and chocolate cookie doughs into a tight cylinder creates beautiful, whimsically swirled cookies with a delicate, intriguing flavor. You can also use the doughs to create playful two-tone checkerboard cookies (see the Variation that follows).

6 tablespoons shelled unsalted pistachio nuts

3 ounces semisweet chocolate, melted and cooled

2 cups unbleached all-purpose flour, plus extra for working the dough

½ teaspoon baking powder

½ teaspoon salt

1 cup (2 sticks) unsalted butter, at room temperature

¾ cup sugar

1 large egg

2 teaspoons pure vanilla extract

1 tablespoon plus 1½ tablespoons unsweetened Dutch-process cocoa powder

1. Place the nuts in a food processor and pulse about 10 times until finely ground (they should look like very

coarse sand); set aside. Combine the flour, baking powder, and salt in a medium bowl.

2. Place the butter and sugar in a large bowl and beat together with an electric mixer on medium-high until fluffy, 2 to 3 minutes. Add the egg and vanilla and beat until smooth. Beat in the flour mixture on low until just incorporated.

3. Divide the dough in half in the bowl. Remove one piece, place it on a sheet of wax paper, and knead in the ground pistachios so they are uniformly distributed. Turn back to the dough still in the bowl and beat into it, on the lowest speed, the melted chocolate and cocoa powder.

4. Divide each piece of dough in half again (you will have four pieces) and press each into a 6-inch square. Wrap each dough square in plastic and refrigerate them for at least 2 hours (or for up to 24 hours).

5. Remove one piece of the pistachio dough and one piece of the chocolate dough from the refrigerator and let them stand on the countertop until soft enough to work, about 15 minutes.

6. Spread a large piece of plastic wrap on a work surface and sprinkle it lightly with flour. Use a lightly floured rolling pin to roll the pistachio dough into a rough 8½-inch square. Using a sharp knife, trim the edges of the dough to create a neat 8-inch square. Repeat with the chocolate dough.

7. Brush the pistachio cookie dough with cold water (about 1 teaspoon). Carefully invert the chocolate cookie dough onto the pistachio cookie dough so that the two doughs are lined up and flush. Use the plastic wrap to push and roll the doughs into a neat, tight log. Tightly wrap the dough in plastic and freeze until firm, about 2 hours. (The dough can be frozen for a longer period; see "A Step Ahead," right.)

8. Repeat Steps 4, 5, and 6 with the remaining pistachio and chocolate doughs.

9. Place the dough logs on the countertop and let stand until softened slightly, about 15 minutes. Meanwhile, preheat the oven to 350°F.

10. Slice the dough into ⅓-inch-thick rounds, rotating it often so it doesn't

>> **A STEP AHEAD**
Dough logs can be wrapped in a double layer of plastic and then a layer of heavy-duty foil and frozen for up to 2 weeks. Defrost the dough in the refrigerator for at least 5 hours or overnight before proceeding as directed from Step 9.

become misshapen as you cut. Place the cookies at least 2 inches apart on ungreased baking sheets.

11. Bake the cookies until they are lightly golden around the edges but still soft on top, about 12 minutes. Let them stand on the baking sheet for 5 minutes and then remove them with a metal spatula to a wire rack to cool completely.

Chocolate-Pistachio Spiral Cookies will keep in an airtight container at room temperature for 3 to 4 days.

VARIATION
Chocolate and Pistachio Checkerboards

Once you've created four neatly trimmed squares of dough, follow these directions to make checkerboards instead of spirals:

1. Brush one piece of the pistachio cookie dough with about 1 teaspoon of cold water. Carefully invert one piece of the chocolate cookie dough onto the pistachio cookie dough so that the two doughs are lined up and flush. Repeat with the remaining pieces of pistachio and chocolate dough. You will have two stacks of dough.

2. Cut one stack of dough into two rectangles. Brush the top of one rectangle with about 1 teaspoon of cold water, and place the second rectangle on top, alternating colors. Repeat with the remaining stack of dough. (Again, you will have two stacks.) Wrap each 4-layered stack in plastic and refrigerate for 1 hour.

3. Remove one stack of cookie dough from the refrigerator and unwrap it. Let it stand on the countertop until softened slightly, about 15 minutes.

4. Using a sharp knife, cut the dough lengthwise into strips about ¼ inch wide. Brush the strips with water and make a stack that is 4 strips high, alternating the direction of the colors as you stack to create a checkerboard pattern. Repeat with the remaining cookie dough. Wrap each of the two stacks in plastic, and chill, slice, and bake as directed from the end of Step 7.

Orange–Cream Cheese Spiral Cookies

Simple to prepare but ridiculously yummy, a great choice for a last-minute swap.

This recipe is an old favorite of mine, not only because the cookies are so pretty to look at and delightfully tender, but because they require just a handful of ingredients, ones that I usually have on hand. The orange flavor is very subtle, really more of a slight tang—it plays beautifully off the cinnamon sugar and the cream cheese–enriched dough. Even if you're not a fan of marmalade, I suggest you give these cookies a whirl—they might just make you a convert!

MAKES: 36 cookies
BAKE TIME:
13 to 16 minutes
QUICK PREP
FREEZE ME!

2 cups unbleached all-purpose flour; plus extra for working the dough

¼ cup plus 2 tablespoons sugar

½ teaspoon salt

8 ounces (1 package) chilled cream cheese, cut into 8 pieces

1 cup (2 sticks) unsalted butter, chilled, cut into 16 pieces

⅔ cup orange marmalade

½ teaspoon ground cinnamon

1. Combine the flour, ¼ cup sugar, and salt in a food processor and pulse to combine. Add the cream cheese and butter and pulse until the mixture resembles coarse meal (do not overprocess).

>> **A STEP AHEAD**
Dough logs can be wrapped in a double layer of plastic and then a layer of heavy-duty foil and frozen for up to 1 month. Defrost the dough in the refrigerator for at least 5 hours or overnight before proceeding as directed from Step 6.

2. Turn the mixture out onto a lightly floured work surface and shape the dough into two 6-inch squares. Wrap the dough squares in plastic and refrigerate for at least 2 hours (or up to 2 days).

3. Place the marmalade in a blender or food processor and blend until smooth. (It won't spread as well if it's not blended.)

4. Remove the dough squares from the refrigerator and let them stand on the countertop until softened slightly, about 15 minutes. Unwrap one square of dough and place it on a lightly floured work surface. With a lightly floured rolling pin, roll it out into a 10-inch square.

5. Spread half of the marmalade evenly over the dough. Roll the dough into a tight log. Wrap the log in plastic wrap and place it in the freezer for 1 hour to firm up. Repeat with the remaining dough square and marmalade. (The dough can be frozen for a longer period; see "A Step Ahead," left.)

6. Place the dough logs on the countertop and let them stand until softened slightly, about 15 minutes. Meanwhile, preheat the oven to 375°F. Line a few baking sheets with parchment paper.

7. Combine the remaining sugar and the cinnamon in a small bowl. Trim the uneven ends from the dough logs. Slice the dough into ½-inch-thick rounds, rotating the dough often so it doesn't become misshapen as you cut.

8. Arrange the cookies about 1 inch apart on the baking sheets and sprinkle liberally with the cinnamon sugar.

9. Bake the cookies until golden brown, 13 to 16 minutes. Transfer the baking sheets to wire racks and let the cookies cool completely on the sheets.

Orange–Cream Cheese Spiral Cookies will keep in an airtight container at room temperature for 3 to 4 days.

Chapter 7

DOUBLE HAPPINESS

LUSCIOUS SANDWICH COOKIES

The poor Earl of Sandwich—when he came up with a smart way to hold messy fillings in the hand, he was limited to bread and probably a sad slice of meat. He didn't know that he could use adorable little cookies to sandwich all sorts of sticky sweets, like fluffy buttercream, silky chocolate ganache, or berry jam. But luckily we know this, and it has made baking, snacking, and swapping so much the better.

When you want to make something a little out of the ordinary for a cookie exchange, the sandwich cookie might be just the thing. Sandwich cookies aren't more difficult to

make than drop, icebox , or rolled cookies, but because they contain a filling chosen to enhance their flavor, they go a little further to please. Crisp, lemony butter cookies are even better when sweetened with strawberry jam. The earthy flavor of walnut cookies is balanced by the sophisticated sweetness of a dried fig compote. A peppermint patty becomes a creamy contrast for two cakey chocolate cookies that enclose it. It's true that when you choose a sandwich cookie recipe you'll need to bake twice as many cookies to meet your required yield, but instead of thinking of this in terms of labor, think of it as a way to double your eating and swapping pleasure.

The neatest sandwich cookies are made with rolled and cut cookies that are identical in size and shape. Make sure the cookies are completely cooled (unless otherwise directed) before filling them, or the filling might melt and run. And take care not to overfill them—you want to use enough buttercream or jam to make a flavor impact, but not so much that the filling will ooze from the edges messily.

Over time, fillings can soften even the crispest cookies, so it's best to sandwich your cookies on the day of the swap. This doesn't mean that you have to do everything at the last minute. Just keep your baked cookies and prepared filling separate and assemble when needed. Fillings that contain dairy, such as buttercream and ganache, are perishable and should be stored in the refrigerator. Chilling these can make them difficult to spread, so be sure to let them come to room temperature (a few hours on the countertop should do the trick) before slathering them between the cookies. Keep these considerations in mind and your sandwich making will go smoothly. The earl would be proud.

Jam-Filled Lemon Sandwich Cookies

Delicate lemony cookies sing "Spring!"

These lemony butter cookies can be served on their own, dusted with confectioners' sugar, but are even better when sandwiched with some strawberry jam. Feel free to play with their shape, as I do—in the spring, I use a duckling or a tulip; for a baby shower, I have a bottle-shaped cutter. Just be sure the cutter is approximately the same size as a 2-inch round cutter, so you wind up with the number of cookies that you need.

Fill the cookies just before you go to your swap (you can make the filling and the cookies a day in advance) so they'll be as fresh as possible when you arrive.

MAKES:
48 sandwich cookies
BAKE TIME:
12 to 15 minutes
FREEZE ME!

2 cups unbleached all-purpose flour, plus extra for working the dough

¼ teaspoon salt

¾ cup (1½ sticks) unsalted butter, at room temperature

⅔ cup sugar

2 tablespoons finely grated lemon zest

1 large egg

1 teaspoon pure vanilla extract

½ cup smooth strawberry jam (see Note)

Confectioners' sugar, for dusting

1. Whisk together the flour and salt in a medium bowl. Set aside.

2. Place the butter, sugar, and lemon zest in a large bowl and beat together with an electric mixer on medium-high until fluffy, 2 to 3 minutes. Add the egg and vanilla and beat until incorporated. Add the flour mixture and mix on low until the dough comes together in a ball.

3. Divide the dough in half and, on a lightly floured work surface with lightly floured hands, press it into two ½-inch-thick disks. Wrap each disk in plastic and refrigerate for at least 2 hours or up to 2 days. (The dough can be frozen at this point; see "A Step Ahead," right.)

 Party On

Spring Fling // WARM(ISH) WEATHER SWAP

It's spring (or if it isn't, go ahead and pretend it is)! Throw open your windows and let in some fresh air! Wear large hats! Rent a bunny (real or otherwise)! Whatever the month, make this the time to shower your senses with crisp, light cookies and refreshing cups of tea. Whip up some Jam-Filled Lemon Sandwich Cookies (dig out your tulip-shaped cookie cutter), and for friends in need of ideas, suggest Green Tea Cookies with Almond Cream Filling (page 114), Blueberry-Almond Biscotti (page 151), and Pistachio Sacristans (page 83). Light and seasonal party fare might include grilled fruit skewers, asparagus spears wrapped in prosciutto, goat-cheese-and-herb crostini, veggies with lemon thyme dip, and cucumber sandwiches. Get your kettle puffing and set up a tea bar next to your cooktop, with mugs, a selection of tea bags, sweeteners, lemon slices, and cream or milk. And don't forget the iced tea (see page 212).

For displaying cookies, buy dime-store Easter baskets. Check out www.efavors.com and www.wedding channelstore.com to score on incredibly inexpensive party favors like teapot tape measures and personalized tea bags (printed with the name of your party and the date). The array of spoon-themed items at The Spoon Sisters (www.spoonsisters.com) might also strike your fancy. White lace gloves are optional.

Oh, and another idea altogether: Evoke springtime in Japan with a cherry blossom (*hanami*) party. Serve vegetable sushi, yakitori (skewers of grilled meat), steamed edamame, wasabi peas, nori crackers, and ginger ice cream. Those green tea cookies should be on the swap table, naturally.

4. Preheat the oven to 375°F. Line several baking sheets with parchment paper.

5. Remove one of the dough disks from the refrigerator and knead it 4 or 5 times on a lightly floured work surface to soften it. With a lightly floured rolling pin, roll out the dough to ⅛-inch thick. Use a 2-inch cookie cutter to cut out as many cookies as you can. Place the cookies about 1 inch apart on the prepared baking sheets. Wrap the scraps in plastic and refrigerate.

6. Bake the cookies until they are set and dry and just beginning to turn golden around the edges, 12 to 15 minutes. Slide the parchment sheet with the cookies onto wire racks and let the cookies cool completely.

7. Roll, cut, and bake the remaining dough (including any scraps), using fresh parchment paper, as directed.

8. To assemble the cookies, use a small offset spatula to spread about ½ teaspoon of jam on half of the cookies. Top with the remaining cookies. Lightly sift some confectioners' sugar over the cookies.

Jam-Filled Lemon Sandwich Cookies will keep, layered between parchment paper, in an airtight container at room temperature for up to 2 days. (Unfilled, the cookies will keep for 3 to 4 days.)

Note: Before measuring the jam, stir it well until any lumps dissolve and it is smooth. Puree it if it is very chunky.

VARIATION

Cream Cheese and Jam–Filled Lemon Cookies

Instead of jam, you can fill these with a richer, creamier frosting reminiscent of that classic favorite, the cream-cheese-and-jelly sandwich: Combine 4 ounces of cream cheese with 2 tablespoons of jam and 2 tablespoons of confectioners' sugar in a small bowl and stir until smooth. Fill as directed in Step 8.

>> **A STEP AHEAD**
The dough can be wrapped in a double layer of plastic and then a layer of heavy-duty foil and frozen for up to 1 month. Defrost it in the refrigerator for at least 5 hours or overnight before proceeding as directed from Step 3.

Green Tea Cookies
with Almond Cream

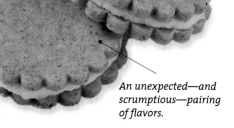

An unexpected—and scrumptious—pairing of flavors.

Ground green tea leaves give these cookies a beautiful speckled appearance and wonderful fragrance. For the filling, I prefer butter for its superior flavor. But if your cookies are going to be kept for a few days after the swap, you might use longer-keeping shortening instead. Also, I suggest filling the sandwiches just before you go to the swap, so the cookies don't soften too much.

FOR THE COOKIES

2 cups unbleached all-purpose flour, plus extra for working the dough

2 tablespoons finely ground green tea leaves (see Note)

½ teaspoon salt

1 cup (2 sticks) unsalted butter, at room temperature

½ cup confectioners' sugar

1 large egg

½ teaspoon pure vanilla extract

FOR THE FILLING

½ cup (1 stick) unsalted butter, at room temperature, or vegetable shortening

2½ cups confectioners' sugar

1 teaspoon pure almond extract

Pinch of salt

1. Make the cookies: Combine the flour, ground green tea, and salt in a medium bowl.

2. Place the butter and ½ cup sugar in a large bowl and beat together with an electric mixer on medium-high until fluffy, 2 to 3 minutes. Add the egg and vanilla and beat until incorporated. Add the flour mixture and mix on low speed until the dough comes together in a ball.

3. Divide the dough in half and, on a lightly floured surface with lightly floured hands, press it into two ½-inch-thick disks. Wrap the disks in plastic and refrigerate them for at least 2 hours or up to 2 days. (The dough can be frozen at this point; see "A Step Ahead," right.)

4. Preheat the oven to 350°F. Line several baking sheets with parchment paper.

5. Remove one of the dough disks from the refrigerator and knead it 4 or 5 times on a lightly floured work surface to soften it. With a lightly floured rolling pin, roll out the dough to a thickness of a scant ¼ inch. Use a 2-inch round cookie cutter to cut out as many circles as you can. Place the cookies about 1 inch apart on the baking sheets. Wrap the scraps in plastic and refrigerate.

6. Bake the cookies until they are set and dry and just beginning to turn golden around the edges, 9 to 12 minutes. Slide the parchment sheets with the cookies onto wire racks and let the cookies cool completely.

7. Roll, cut, and bake the remaining dough (including any scraps), using fresh parchment paper, as directed.

8. Make the filling: Put the butter and 2½ cups confectioners' sugar in a large bowl and beat together with an electric mixer on low until combined. Beat in the almond extract and salt. Add 1½ teaspoons water and beat on high until light and fluffy, about 5 minutes.

9. Spoon a teaspoon of the filling onto half of the cookies. Top with the remaining cookies.

Green Tea Cookies with Almond Cream will keep in an airtight container at room temperature for up to 2 days. (Unfilled, the cookies will keep for 3 to 4 days.)

Note: Ground green tea leaves are available at natural foods markets (I prefer the matcha variety). If you can't find them, simply grind the leaves from about 4 tea bags of green tea in a coffee grinder.

>> A STEP AHEAD

The dough can be wrapped in a double layer of plastic and then a layer of heavy-duty foil and frozen for up to 1 month. Defrost it in the refrigerator for at least 5 hours or overnight before proceeding as directed from Step 4.

Walnut Sandwiches with Fig Filling

Almost like a homemade Fig Newton— but better.

MAKES: 36 sandwich cookies
BAKE TIME: 12 to 15 minutes
QUICK PREP
FREEZE ME!

A little whole wheat flour in the dough gives these cookies a wholesome graham cracker–like flavor. For a more refined cookie, you could replace it with white flour. When you cook the figs, watch them carefully toward the end—just a little liquid should remain in the pot, so the filling is moist but not watery.

FOR THE COOKIES

1 cup walnuts

¾ cup sugar

2 cups unbleached all-purpose flour, plus extra for working the dough

½ cup whole wheat flour

½ teaspoon salt

1 cup (2 sticks) unsalted butter, at room temperature

1 large egg

FOR THE FILLING

8 ounces dried Calimyrna figs (about 12), tough stems removed, chopped

¼ cup sugar

½ peel from an orange, preferably organic

1. Make the cookies: Combine the walnuts and ¼ cup of the sugar in a food processor and process, pulsing 8 to 10 times, until the nuts are finely ground (the mixture should resemble very coarse sand). Transfer the mixture to a bowl and whisk in the flours and salt.

2. Place the butter and the remaining ½ cup sugar in a large bowl and beat together with an electric mixer on

medium-high until fluffy, 2 to 3 minutes. Add the egg and beat until incorporated. Add the flour mixture and beat on low until the dough comes together in a ball.

3. Divide the dough in half and, on a lightly floured surface with lightly floured hands, press it into two ½-inch-thick disks. Wrap the disks in plastic and refrigerate them for at least 2 hours or up to 2 days. (The dough can be frozen at this point; see "A Step Ahead," right.)

4. Make the fig filling: Combine the figs, sugar, orange peel, and 1 cup of water in a medium saucepan over high heat and bring to a boil. Reduce the heat to low and simmer, uncovered, until the figs are soft and have absorbed most of the liquid, about 20 minutes. Place the figs in a food processor and process until smooth. Set aside to cool completely.

5. Preheat the oven to 350°F. Line a baking sheet with parchment paper.

6. Remove one of the dough disks from the refrigerator and knead it 4 or 5 times on a lightly floured work surface to soften it. With a lightly floured rolling pin, roll out the dough to a thickness of a scant ¼ inch. Use a 2-inch round cookie cutter to cut out as many circles as you can. Place the cookies on the baking sheet about 1 inch apart. Wrap the scraps in plastic and refrigerate.

7. Bake the cookies until they are set and dry, 12 to 15 minutes. Slide the entire parchment sheet with the cookies onto a wire rack and let the cookies cool completely.

8. Repeat steps 6 and 7 with the remaining disk of dough (and any scraps), using fresh parchment paper.

9. To assemble the cookies, use a small offset spatula to spread about ½ teaspoon of the fig mixture on half of the cookies. Top with the remaining cookies.

Walnut Sandwiches with Fig Filling will keep at room temperature in an airtight container for up to 2 days.

VARIATION

Although homemade fig filling is delicious, any type of jam or preserves could be substituted to save time. Orange marmalade or apricot preserves would be especially good with the whole wheat and walnuts. If you can find good-quality fig jam (look for an artisan variety; most supermarket brands don't taste like fig at all!), use that.

» A STEP AHEAD

The dough disks can be wrapped in a double layer of plastic and then a layer of heavy-duty foil and frozen for up to 1 month. Defrost them in the refrigerator for at least 5 hours or overnight before proceeding as directed from Step 4.

Mini Hazelnut Linzer Hearts

Bake some linzers and spread the love!

MAKES: 36 small sandwich cookies

BAKE TIME: 10 to 12 minutes

QUICK PREP

FREEZE ME!

Linzer sandwiches are so rich that larger cookies often go half-eaten. But bite-size Linzer hearts give you all the Viennese-style decadence of a big cookie with half the guilt (which—let's be honest—means you can eat more of them!). These cookies are made with two sizes of cookie cutters—a larger heart to cut out the cookies and a smaller one to create the window; you can find them at Williams-Sonoma or N.Y. Cake & Baking Distributor (where the small ones are sold in a set of aspic cutters; see Resources, page 216).

1 cup skinned hazelnuts (see page 120)

⅔ cup granulated sugar

1 cup (2 sticks) unsalted butter, at room temperature

1 large egg yolk

1 teaspoon pure vanilla extract

2⅔ cups unbleached all-purpose flour, plus extra for working the dough

¼ teaspoon salt

¼ cup seedless raspberry jam

Confectioners' sugar, for dusting

1. Place the hazelnuts and ⅓ cup of the sugar in a food processor and pulse 8 to 10 times until very finely ground (the mixture should resemble very coarse sand).

2. Place the butter and the remaining ⅓ cup of the sugar in a large mixing bowl and beat together with an electric mixer on medium-high speed until fluffy, 2 to 3 minutes. Add the egg yolk and vanilla and beat until incorporated. Add the flour, salt, and the hazelnut mixture and mix on low speed until the dough comes together in a ball.

3. Divide the dough into three parts and, on a lightly floured surface with lightly floured hands, press it into three ½-inch-thick disks. Wrap the disks in plastic and refrigerate them for at least 2 hours or up to 2 days. (The dough may be frozen at this point; see "A Step Ahead," right.)

4. Preheat the oven to 350°F. Line several baking sheets with parchment paper.

5. Remove one of the dough disks from the refrigerator and knead it 4 or 5 times on a lightly floured work surface to soften it. With a lightly floured rolling pin, roll out the dough to a thickness of a scant ¼ inch. Use a 1½-inch heart-shaped cutter to cut out as many hearts as you can. Place the hearts on the prepared baking sheets and use a smaller heart-shaped cutter to cut a peek-a-boo center into half of the cookies. Alternatively, use a skewer to poke holes in half of the cookies. (These holes should be in rows, about ¼-inch apart from each other.)

6. Bake the cookies until they are lightly golden, 10 to 12 minutes. Slide the parchment sheets with the cookies onto wire racks and let the cookies cool completely.

7. Roll, cut, and bake the remaining disks of dough (and any scraps), using fresh parchment paper, as directed.

8. To assemble the cookies, use a small offset spatula to spread about ¼ teaspoon of jam on each of the un-poked hearts; spread the jam to within ⅛ inch of the edge. Lightly sift some confectioners' sugar over the poked hearts and place each on top of the jam-covered hearts.

Mini Hazelnut Linzer Hearts will keep, layered between parchment paper, in an airtight container at room temperature for up to 2 days.

>> **A STEP AHEAD**
The dough can be wrapped in a double layer of plastic and then a layer of heavy-duty foil and frozen for up to 1 month. Defrost it in the refrigerator for at least 5 hours or overnight before proceeding as directed from Step 4.

VARIATION
Hazelnut–Milk Chocolate Sandwiches

These cookies are just as good sandwiched with milk chocolate ganache. To make enough ganache to fill one recipe of cookies, place ½ cup (3 ounces) of milk chocolate chips and 1 teaspoon of unsweetened Dutch-process or regular cocoa powder in a heat-proof bowl. Bring ½ cup of heavy cream to a boil in a small saucepan and pour it over the chocolate. Cover the bowl with plastic wrap and let it stand for 5 minutes. Whisk the ganache until it is smooth, then let it cool until it is thickened but still spreadable, about 30 minutes, before filling the cookies.

Ganache is easy to make, but if you're really strapped for time, you can take an undeniably delicious shortcut and use Nutella as a filling.

SMART COOKIE

Get the Skinny   HOW TO SKIN HAZELNUTS

The conventional method for skinning hazelnuts is to roast them in an oven at 325°F for 15 to 20 minutes, wrap them in a clean kitchen towel to steam for a few minutes, and then rub them vigorously in the towel until the skins fall away. While I've had some success with this method, I'm never completely satisfied with the significant proportion of stubborn skin that clings to the nuts. And the mess from the flakes of skin can be truly horrendous. Lately I've using another technique that works so well I'm shocked it isn't more widely known: Place the hazelnuts in a saucepan and cover them with water to a depth of 1 inch. Add a tablespoon of baking soda and bring to a boil for 3 minutes. Strain the nuts under cold running water, rubbing them between your palms. The skins will completely dissolve. Pat the hazelnuts dry before using them.

Since these nuts are not oven-toasted, you may want to roast them to bring out their flavor. Place the dried, skinned hazelnuts on a baking sheet and bake them at 325°F until they're golden brown and fragrant, 15 minutes or so.

Chocolate-Mint Sandwich Cookies

There's a hidden treasure in each cookie!

When I set out to make these cookies, I started with the idea that I would just sandwich a Peppermint Pattie between two warm chocolate rounds and leave it at that. But my dough spread in the oven, and when I made my sandwiches the candies were lost inside the cookies instead of becoming a filling visible at the edges. What to do? I got out a biscuit cutter and pressed it down on the cookie sandwiches, cutting away the excess around the edges and sealing the candy inside. The creamy peppermint was now a hidden surprise. Fabulous! This is my new favorite cookie, hands down.

MAKES:
32 sandwich cookies
BAKE TIME:
10 to 12 minutes
FREEZE ME!

2 cups unbleached all-purpose flour

¾ cup unsweetened Dutch-process cocoa powder, sifted

½ teaspoon baking soda

½ teaspoon salt

1¼ cup (2½ sticks) unsalted butter, at room temperature

2 cups sugar

2 large eggs

1½ teaspoons pure vanilla extract

32 mini York Peppermint Pattie candies

1. Preheat the oven to 350°F. Line several baking sheets with parchment paper.

>> **A STEP AHEAD**
The dropped dough can be frozen on the baking sheets, transferred to ziplock plastic freezer bags, and stored in the freezer for up to 1 month. Transfer frozen dough to ungreased baking sheets and bake a minute or two longer than directed.

2. Combine the flour, cocoa powder, baking soda, and salt in a medium bowl.

3. Place the butter and sugar in a large bowl and beat together with an electric mixer on medium until fluffy, 2 to 3 minutes. Add the eggs and vanilla and beat until smooth. Beat in the flour mixture on low until just combined.

4. Roll scant tablespoonfuls of dough between the palms of your hands to form small balls. Place them 3 inches apart on the prepared baking sheets. (The dough can be frozen at this point; see "A Step Ahead," left.)

5. Bake the cookies until they are dry on top, 10 to 12 minutes. Let them stand on the baking sheet for 3 to 4 minutes to cool slightly.

6. Working quickly, and while the cookies are still warm, sandwich a peppermint pattie between two cookies and transfer the sandwich to a wire rack to cool. Repeat with the remaining patties and cookies. Then, while the cookies are still pretty soft, place each sandwich on a cutting board and use a 2-inch biscuit cutter to press down on it, cutting away the edges and sealing the peppermint pattie inside.

Chocolate-Mint Sandwich Cookies will keep in an airtight container at room temperature for 3 to 4 days.

Chapter 8

PLAY DOUGH

SHAPED AND CUT COOKIES

I f you've ever needed a reason to play with your food, this is it. The cookies in this chapter all tap into your inner Rembrandt *and* your inner Peter Pan. You can get creative shaping dough by hand, or by icing rolled and cut cookies and decorating them with sprinkles, colored sugar, edible glitter, and whatever else strikes your fancy. Sure, these cookies take some time to make, but the effort shows: Dark chocolate shortbread made to look like dominoes; vanilla pretzels sprinkled with rainbow-colored sanding sugar; puffy sesame cookies that look like giant Pac-Men; dapper gingerbread men in their holiday finest . . . If you want to make some attention-grabbing cookies, look no further.

The doughs that are shaped by hand are pretty forgiving and easy to work with, but there's a bit more to making cookies that must be rolled out, then cut. It's a fun project, and one that's entirely manageable if broken down into steps over the course of a few days or weeks:

* **Make the dough.** This should only take minutes with an electric mixer. Once your dough is made, wrap it tightly in plastic and refrigerate it for up to 2 days. (At this point you can also freeze it for a longer period following the directions in the recipe.)

* **Once your dough is well-chilled** it is ready to roll. If it's been in the refrigerator for longer than 2 hours, it may be hard and a little bit crumbly at first. Don't worry. Break it into smaller pieces and knead it a few times on a lightly floured countertop to soften it up. (Conversely, if the dough is too soft and sticky to roll out, you'll need to chill it for a little longer.) As you roll the dough, make sure to rotate it often, frequently sliding a large offset spatula underneath to make sure it isn't sticking to the counter.

* **Cut out your cookies** and place them on a parchment-lined baking sheet. If you find that dough sticks to the cutter, try dusting it with a bit of flour (and be sure to wipe off any nubbins of dough that adhere to the cutter—they can make a mess of things). Reserve the dough scraps and re-roll them until you have used all of the dough.

* **The baked cookies can be decorated** as soon as they have cooled completely, or you can pack them away in airtight containers and ice them up to a day later if that's more convenient. For both hand-shaped and rolled cookies, you'll want to pack them between sheets of parchment or wax paper to protect any decorative doodads.

Chocolate Shortbread Dominoes

Finally, food you can really *play with!*

These cookies, shaped and decorated like dominoes, beg to be baked for a game night swap. My kids love to play games with them before gobbling them up. If you have similarly enthusiastic eaters, make sure to use every possible number combination on the cookies, so they can use the whole batch (see Note).

MAKES: 48 cookies
BAKE TIME:
12 to 14 minutes
FREEZE ME!

1½ cups unbleached all-purpose flour, plus extra for rolling the dough

⅔ cup unsweetened Dutch-process cocoa powder

1 teaspoon kosher salt

1 cup (2 sticks) unsalted butter, at room temperature

1 cup confectioners' sugar

1 teaspoon pure vanilla extract

½ cup M&M's Minis

1. Combine the flour, cocoa powder, and salt in a medium bowl. Place the butter and sugar in a large bowl and beat together with an electric mixer on medium until fluffy, about 3 minutes. Beat in the vanilla. Beat in the flour mixture on low until the dough is smooth.

2. Divide the dough in half. Lay some plastic wrap underneath each piece

>> **A STEP AHEAD**

The dough can be wrapped in a double layer of plastic and then a layer of heavy-duty foil and frozen for up to 1 month. Defrost it in the refrigerator for at least 5 hours or overnight before proceeding as directed from Step 3.

Got Game?

OLD-SCHOOL GAMES 'N' SWAP

Cookies can make you feel like a kid again, so why not indulge your inner adolescent by combining a cookie exchange with game night? Set out your favorite board games—Scrabble, Parcheesi, Yahtzee, Trivial Pursuit—or round up some party games like Catch Phrase and Balderdash. Provide submarine sandwiches, tons of potato chips, and soft drinks in old-fashioned glass bottles. Make some Chocolate Shortbread Dominoes for the swap, and decorate the table with fuzzy dice, which can be claimed as party favors later. Don't have a fuzzy-dice shop in your town? Check out the incredible variety at www .fuzzythis.com.

and press each into a 6-inch square. Wrap the plastic around each square of dough and refrigerate for 30 minutes. (The dough can be frozen at this point; see "A Step Ahead," page 125.)

3. Preheat the oven to 350°F. Line two baking sheets with parchment paper.

4. Working with one piece of dough at a time (keep the other refrigerated), roll out the dough to a ⅛-inch thickness on a lightly floured work surface using a lightly floured rolling pin. Be sure to turn the dough often so it doesn't stick.

5. Use a sharp paring knife and a ruler to cut the dough into 1½-by-3-inch rectangles, rerolling scraps and recutting until all of the dough is used. Transfer the cookies to one of the prepared baking sheets, leaving about 1 inch between each cookie. Use the dull edge of the knife to make an indentation widthwise across the middle of each cookie.

6. Arrange M&M's Minis on top of the cookies so the cookies resemble dominoes, pressing on the candies lightly so they adhere.

7. Bake the cookies until they are firm, 12 to 14 minutes. Slide the entire parchment sheet with the cookies to a wire rack and let them cool completely. Repeat with the remaining dough square and the second prepared baking sheet.

Chocolate Shortbread Dominoes will keep in an airtight container at room temperature for 2 to 3 days.

Note: For reference on how to arrange the M&M's to resemble dominoes, and to learn how to play the game itself, visit www.domino-games.com.

Sesame and Ginger Munchers

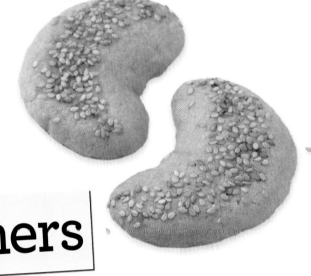

The first time I made these cookies, I thought they would look like crescent moons. However, I added so much butter and tahini to the luscious dough that in the oven the cookies spread, and ended up looking like crescent moons—crossed with Pac-Man. But everyone who tried them was delighted by their shape as well as their rich, nutty sesame flavor (enhanced by a crunchy coating of sesame seeds), so I just pretended the '80s arcade-game nod was intentional. In the end, we were all happy.

MAKES: 48 cookies
BAKE TIME:
10 to 12 minutes
QUICK PREP
FREEZE ME!

2 cups unbleached all-purpose flour

1 teaspoon baking soda

½ teaspoon salt

½ teaspoon ground ginger

1 cup (2 sticks) unsalted butter, at room temperature

½ cup granulated sugar

½ cup packed light brown sugar

1 large egg

1 teaspoon pure vanilla extract

¾ cup tahini (sesame paste; see box, page 128)

¼ cup sesame seeds

1. Preheat the oven to 350°F. Line several baking sheets with parchment paper.

2. Combine the flour, baking soda, salt, and ginger in a medium bowl.

3. Place the butter and sugars in a large bowl and beat together with an electric mixer on medium until fluffy, about 3 minutes. Add the egg, vanilla, and tahini and beat until smooth. Beat in the flour mixture on low until just combined. Refrigerate the dough to firm it up, 10 minutes.

4. Place the sesame seeds in a small bowl. Scoop up tablespoonfuls of dough and roll them between your palms to form balls. Shape each ball into a crescent, with ends that are thinner than the middle. Dip the tops in the sesame seeds. Place the crescents seeded-side up on the prepared baking sheets, leaving about 3 inches between each cookie. (The cookies can be frozen at this point; see "A Step Ahead," left.)

5. Bake the cookies until they are just set, 10 to 12 minutes. Let them stand on the baking sheets for 5 minutes and then carefully slide the parchment sheet with the cookies to wire racks and let them cool completely.

Sesame and Ginger Munchers will keep in an airtight container at room temperature for 3 to 4 days.

SMART COOKIE

Sesame Street   SESAME SEEDS AND TAHINI

There are three different types of sesame seeds that you may see at the market: brown, black, and white. Brown and black sesame seeds can be used interchangeably (some people say that the black ones have a more robust flavor, but I can't tell the difference). I usually buy brown seeds, which are actually more of a tan or khaki color, because I think they look better in desserts. White sesame seeds are simply brown sesame seeds that have been hulled. They will work in cookie recipes, but I prefer unhulled seeds, which have more nutrients.

Some cookie recipes call for tahini, a paste made from hulled, toasted sesame seeds. It's the sesame-seed equivalent of peanut butter, and imparts a nutty flavor and rich texture to baked goods. Tahini can be found in the ethnic food aisle at most supermarkets, and also at natural foods supermarkets and Middle Eastern food stores. This thick sesame paste tends to separate, so before measuring it, be sure to stir it well until the oil is incorporated.

Maple-Walnut Wedding Cakes

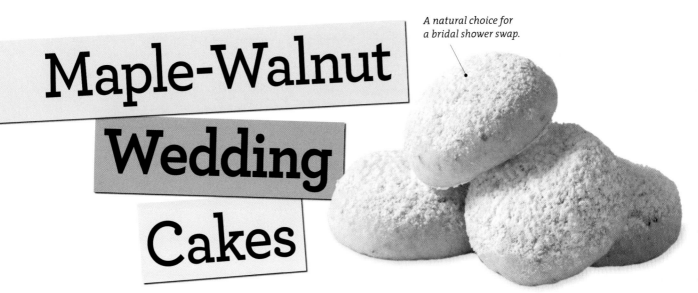

A natural choice for a bridal shower swap.

Traditional Mexican wedding cakes are among the world's most beloved cookies, for their dense, tender texture as well as their comforting, simple flavor. Made with ground nuts, flour, butter, and sugar, they have a slight crunch when you bite into them, but then almost instantly melt in your mouth. Adding a little maple syrup and some maple extract give these traditional cookies a slightly untraditional spin, one that really highlights their flavor and texture.

MAKES: 36 cookies
BAKE TIME: 18 to 20 minutes
QUICK PREP

1½ cups walnuts

2¼ cups unbleached all-purpose flour

1 teaspoon salt

1 cup (2 sticks) unsalted butter,
   at room temperature

½ cup granulated sugar

2 teaspoons pure maple syrup

1 teaspoon pure vanilla extract

½ teaspoon pure maple extract

6 tablespoons confectioners' sugar

1. Preheat the oven to 325°F. Line several baking sheets with parchment paper.

2. Place the walnuts in a food processor and pulse 5 to 8 times until

they are finely chopped (they should resemble very coarse sand). Combine the chopped nuts, flour, and salt in a medium bowl and set aside.

3. Place the butter and sugar in a large bowl and beat together with an electric mixer on medium-high

until fluffy, 2 to 3 minutes. Beat the maple syrup and vanilla and maple extracts into the butter mixture until incorporated. Beat in the nut mixture on low until just combined.

4. Scoop up tablespoonfuls of dough and roll them between your palms

Reality Bytes // VIRTUAL COOKIE SWAP

Sometimes life just gets in the way of the cookie. If you're pressed for time, or if your favorite bakers live across the country, consider the virtual cookie swap. It's easy to plan and host, although not quite as tasty: In a virtual swap, participants exchange recipes instead of cookies.

A few online venues lend themselves to easy exchanging. Social networking sites like Facebook can make swapping a breeze. If all of your participants are Facebookers, start a group and begin inviting people. Swappers can record their recipes in separate posts and strike up witty banter on the wall. Additionally, many online cookie swaps take place in the blogosphere. Either use the comments feature on an already established blog, or make a communal blog and allow all participants access to it to post their recipes. Suggest video and picture uploads for a personal touch.

For a more controlled virtual exchange, send e-mail invitations to your friends and family explaining your request—ask for a recipe, a photo, and a description of their cookie. Once you've received everyone's contribution, you can begin compiling. Use Tastebook (www.tastebook .com) or a similar site to publish your homemade cookbook and fill the recipe pages with photos from the swappers and notes about their delicacies. Or, simply put the recipes and extras in a document to be e-mailed around. Whether elaborate or simple, these recipe collections are a sweet way to help a bride or recent graduate mark a new chapter in her life. And they're an ideal place to assemble generations of recipes for a family reunion, or in memoriam of a loved one.

With so many options, a cookie swap can be just a click away.

to form balls. Place the balls on the prepared baking sheets, leaving 1½ inches between each cookie.

5. Bake the cookies until they are cooked through but not dry and just barely golden around the bottom edges, 18 to 20 minutes. Slide the cookies, still on the parchment paper, onto wire racks to cool.

6. Place the confectioners' sugar in a shallow bowl. When the cookies are completely cooled, dip each one in the sugar to coat.

Maple-Walnut Wedding Cakes will keep in an airtight container at room temperature for 3 to 4 days.

VARIATION
Mexican Wedding Cakes

To make the traditional version of these cookies, substitute pecans for the walnuts, water for the maple syrup, omit the maple extract, and increase the vanilla to 1½ teaspoons.

Vanilla Pretzels

To mimic a real pretzel, try the chocolate variation.

MAKES:
36 pretzel cookies

BAKE TIME:
15 minutes

FREEZE ME!

These snack-inspired cookies aren't difficult to make, although the rolling and shaping does take some time. But if you like using your hands, you won't mind the process one bit; in fact you'll enjoy it—it's a lot like playing with clay. Don't skip the multicolored sanding sugar, which looks like cartoon-colored coarse salt. Not only does it make the cookies beautiful, it adds necessary sweetness and crunch.

2¼ cups unbleached all-purpose flour, plus extra for rolling the dough

½ teaspoon baking powder

¼ teaspoon salt

½ cup (1 stick) unsalted butter, at room temperature

¼ cup granulated sugar

1 large egg

1 teaspoon pure vanilla extract

3 tablespoons milk

1 large egg yolk, lightly beaten

6 tablespoons coarse multicolored sanding sugar (see Resources, page 216)

1. Combine the flour, baking powder, and salt in a medium mixing bowl.

2. Place the butter and sugar in a large bowl and beat together with an electric mixer on medium-high until fluffy, 2 to 3 minutes. Add the egg, vanilla, and milk and beat until smooth. With the mixer on low,

gradually add the flour mixture until it is all incorporated. Turn the mixer to medium and beat until the dough is smooth.

3. Lay a piece of plastic wrap on a work surface and turn the dough out onto it. Press the dough into a 6-inch square, wrap it, and refrigerate it for at least 2 hours or for up to 1 day.

4. Preheat the oven to 350°F. Line several baking sheets with parchment paper.

5. Use a sharp chef's knife to cut the dough square into 4 equal strips. Cut each strip widthwise into 9 pieces. Roll each piece between your palms to form a ball. On a lightly floured work surface, roll each ball into an 8-inch-long rope. Form each rope into a pretzel shape. Place the pretzels on the prepared baking sheets, leaving

at least 2 inches between cookies. (The dough can be frozen at this point; see "A Step Ahead," right.)

6. Brush the cookies with the egg yolk and sprinkle liberally with sanding sugar. Bake until the cookies are golden and firm, about 15 minutes. Slide the parchment sheets with the cookies onto wire racks and let the cookies cool completely.

Vanilla Pretzels will keep in an airtight container at room temperature for 3 to 4 days.

VARIATION
Chocolate Pretzels

To make a chocolate version, use 1¾ cups of flour and add ½ cup of unsweetened Dutch-process cocoa powder in Step 1. Go with coarse white sanding sugar for sprinkling if you want them to look like the real thing.

>> **A STEP AHEAD**

The dough pretzels can be frozen on the baking sheets, transferred to ziplock freezer bags, and stored in the freezer for up to 1 month. Transfer the frozen dough pretzels to parchment-lined baking sheets, brush with beaten egg yolk and sprinkle with sanding sugar as directed in Step 6, and bake a minute or two longer than directed.

Milk Chocolate–Coconut Shortbread

MAKES: 48 cookies
BAKE TIME:
30 minutes

I **love this recipe** not only for its divine combination of coconut and milk chocolate, but for its pat-in-the-pan ease. Be sure to fully cut the dough *before* baking the cookies, so they'll break apart easily. Use a small offset spatula to lift the first few baked cookies off of the parchment and carefully separate them. After that, breaking up the rest will be a breeze.

2½ cups unbleached all-purpose flour

½ cup confectioners' sugar

½ teaspoon salt

1¼ cups (2½ sticks) unsalted butter, chilled and cut into small pieces

1¼ cups sweetened flaked coconut

1 teaspoon pure vanilla extract

¼ teaspoon pure coconut extract

½ cup milk chocolate chips

1. Preheat the oven to 325°F. Line a 15 x 10 x 1 inch rimmed baking sheet (a jelly roll pan) with parchment paper.

2. Put the flour, confectioners' sugar, and salt in a food processor and pulse once or twice to combine. Add the butter, coconut, and vanilla and coconut extracts and process until the dough comes together in a ball.

3. Turn the dough out (it will be a little crumbly) onto the prepared baking sheet and press it into an even layer. Use a sharp paring knife to cut the dough into 48 pieces, first making 3 lengthwise cuts and then 11 widthwise cuts. Prick the dough all over with a fork. Bake until the shortbread at the edges of the baking sheet are just beginning to turn golden, about 30 minutes.

4. Transfer the baking sheet to a wire rack and let the shortbread cool completely. Break the bars into pieces along the precut lines.

5. Line another baking sheet with parchment paper. Transfer the individual bars to the prepared baking sheet.

6. Place the chocolate chips in a microwave-safe bowl and microwave on high until almost melted, 30 seconds to 1 minute, depending on the strength of your microwave. Stir until smooth. (Alternatively, heat water to a depth of 1 inch in the bottom of a double boiler or a large saucepan and bring to a bare simmer. Place two-thirds of the chocolate in the top of the double boiler or in a stainless steel bowl big enough to rest on top of the saucepan without touching the water. Heat, whisking occasionally, until the chocolate is just melted. Remove from the heat, add in the remaining chocolate, and stir until melted and smooth.)

7. Transfer the chocolate to a medium ziplock bag. Snip a small hole in one corner of the bag and, holding it as you would a pastry bag, pipe free-form lines onto the cookies. Let the chocolate harden, about 30 minutes, before serving.

Milk Chocolate–Coconut Shortbread will keep, layered between parchment paper, in an airtight container at room temperature for 3 to 4 days.

VARIATION
Coconut-Citrus Shortbread

Add a teaspoon each of lime, lemon, and orange zest to the food processor along with the butter. For the decoration, use semisweet or bittersweet chocolate chips, which have a more piquant flavor that better complements the citrus.

SMART COOKIE

The Hole Story
HOW SHORTBREAD GOT ITS SPOTS

Shortbread is pricked all over before baked not only to give the cookies their traditional decoration, but also to allow steam to escape the dough during baking, which prevents it from bubbling up in the oven.

Rolled Vanilla
Cookies
with Royal Icing

When using different cutters, aim for similar sizes so all of the cookies bake uniformly.

MAKES: 48 two-inch or 24 four-inch cookies

BAKE TIME: 7 to 9 minutes

QUICK PREP

FREEZE ME!

This dough is just perfect for cutout cookies. It rolls out easily and smoothly. Once baked, it is melt-in-your-mouth delicious but still sturdy enough to withstand icing. The dough scraps reroll beautifully, so just keep cutting cookies until the dough is gone. However, try not to cut it thinner than ⅛ of an inch—thinner than this and the baked cookies will burn quickly and be brittle.

1 cup (2 sticks) **unsalted butter,** at room temperature

½ cup **sugar**

1 large **egg yolk**

1 teaspoon **pure vanilla extract**

2¼ cups **unbleached all-purpose flour,** plus extra for rolling the dough

¼ teaspoon **salt**

1 recipe **Royal Icing (recipe follows)**

1. Place the butter and sugar in a large bowl and beat together with an electric mixer on medium-high until fluffy, 2 to 3 minutes. Add the egg yolk and vanilla and beat until incorporated, scraping down the sides of the bowl as necessary. Add the flour and salt and mix on low until the dough comes together in a ball.

2. Divide the dough into 3 equal balls. Wrap each ball in plastic and refrigerate it for at least 2 hours or up to 2 days. (The dough can be frozen at this point; see "A Step Ahead," right)

3. Preheat the oven to 375°F. Line several baking sheets with parchment.

4. Remove one ball from the refrigerator and knead it 4 or 5 times on a lightly floured work surface to soften it. With a lightly floured rolling pin, roll out the dough to a thickness of ⅛ inch. Cut it into the desired shapes and place it on the prepared baking sheets. Knead together the

>> **A STEP AHEAD**

The dough can be wrapped in a double layer of plastic and then a layer of heavy-duty foil and frozen for up to 1 month. Defrost it in the refrigerator for at least 5 hours or overnight before proceeding as directed from Step 3.

CALLING CARDS :: SIGNATURE COOKIE CUTTERS

You may already be famous for your pecan sandies or your snickerdoodles. But if you're still searching for the cookie that will make you a coveted guest at the next neighborhood swap, you may want to think in terms of shape instead of recipe.

I'd been making rolled vanilla, chocolate, and gingerbread cookies for years—ghosts and bats for Halloween, hearts for Valentine's Day, stars for Christmas. People liked them, but did they rave? Not really. It wasn't until I was browsing online at www.coppergifts.com that I understood how a rolled-and-cut cookie could be a calling card. It was on page 28 (out of 41 pages of copper cutters) that I saw the poodle. I was immediately captivated by the idea of making cookies in the image of my dog, Mila. Not only did I order the cutter, but I added a jar of black edible glitter and a new gel food coloring set to my cart. Somehow, when I baked my chocolate poodle cookies they looked and tasted better than my hearts and stars ever did. People went crazy for them.

I've since returned to CopperGifts to buy a running gingerbread man (I like to put him in Royal Icing running shorts and write the name of my hometown, "Sag Harbor," across his tank top) and a cutter in the shape of the state of New York (I cover these cookies with white icing and then pipe on Yankee pinstripes—sorry, Boston!). Look for a cookie cutter that will tell people who you are. A sailor? Choose an anchor. A Texan? There's a great longhorn. A Miles Davis fan? Grab the trumpet. With a signature cookie cutter, you'll get more compliments and have more fun than you've ever had making pumpkins or candy canes.

scraps, wrap them in plastic, and refrigerate them.

5. Bake the cookies until they are firm and golden around the edges, 7 to 9 minutes. Slide the parchment sheets with the cookies onto wire racks and let the cookies cool completely.

6. Repeat Steps 4 and 5, using fresh parchment paper, with the remaining balls of dough and the scraps.

7. When the cookies are cool, decorate them with the Royal Icing as directed. Let the iced cookies stand until the icing has hardened, about 30 minutes.

Rolled Vanilla Cookies with Royal Icing will keep, layered between parchment paper, in an airtight container at room temperature for up to 5 days.

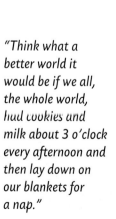

"Think what a better world it would be if we all, the whole world, had cookies and milk about 3 o'clock every afternoon and then lay down on our blankets for a nap."

BARBARA JORDAN

Royal Icing

This smooth, shiny icing—a traditional topping for gingerbread houses and Christmas cookies—can be spread or piped on any rolled cookies. Meringue powder (see Note) or powdered egg whites make this icing fluffy without the worry associated with consuming raw egg whites.

MAKES: enough to decorate 48 small or 24 large rolled cookies

2 tablespoons meringue powder or powdered egg whites (see Note)

5 tablespoons warm water

2 cups confectioners' sugar

Food coloring (optional)

1. Combine the meringue powder and water in a medium bowl. With an electric mixer fitted with the whisk attachment, beat the mixture on high until soft peaks form, 1 to 2 minutes. Add the confectioners' sugar and beat until the icing is shiny and smooth, 3 to 5 minutes. Add extra water as necessary to achieve a spreadable consistency (it should be looser than cake frosting, but not runny).

2. If you'd like to tint the icing different colors, divide it among bowls and stir in various shades of food coloring as desired. Use immediately, or press plastic wrap onto the surface of the icing (otherwise the icing will begin to harden) and refrigerate it until you are ready to use it, for up to 1 day.

3. Spread the icing on cooled cookies with a small offset spatula or craft stick, and/or place it in a pastry bag fitted with a small, plain tip (or a ziplock bag with a small hole snipped in one corner) and pipe it decoratively onto the cookies. Let iced cookies stand until the icing sets up, 30 minutes.

Note: Meringue powder is available at Williams-Sonoma stores, and also from the Baker's Catalogue (www.bakerscatalogue.com). Dried egg whites will work in a pinch, but meringue powder is preferred.

Let's Play Dress Up EMBELLISHING CUTOUT COOKIES

Who says royal icing has to be white? Feel free to play around with different colors and patterns, or try some of these simple ideas:

✳ Add shine with sanding sugar, edible glitter, or shimmery luster dust: Apply any (or all) to just-iced cookies (use a small paint brush to apply luster dust). Work over a rimmed baking sheet to catch any wayward bits, and keep in mind that edible glitter is just like craft glitter—if it spills, you'll have to live with traces of it forever. If you're making dozens of cookies, don't ice all of them before beginning to apply your sugar decorations, or the icing you applied to the first cookies will have already dried by the time you are done with the last. Instead ice first and embellish second, then move on to the next cookie.

✳ Add food coloring to take things up a notch. A set of twelve gel food colors is inexpensive and will last for months if not years. And the quality and variety of the gel colors—Teal! Sky blue! Fuschia!— are a major upgrade from what you'll get from the liquid food coloring sold at the supermarket.

✳ Sprinkles are a quick way to add color. In addition to the standard rainbow and chocolate, you can find themed colors and shapes for many occasions and times of year (autumn leaves, shamrocks, patriotic stars, baby shoes, dinosaurs . . .). Nonpareils give iced cookies a nice snap, and silver dragées, though expensive, class up any cookie. Add all of these as you would glitter or sanding sugar, while the icing is still damp.

✳ Make polka dots, stripes, or plaid: Scrape a small amount of contrasting colored icing into a pastry bag fitted with a small round tip (or a ziplock bag with a small hole snipped in one corner) and dot or line your iced cookies all over.

✳ Marbleize it: Ice your cookies with one color and, while this color is still wet, pipe thin stripes of a second color on top. Drag a toothpick across the stripes, dragging some of the second color across the first for a marbled effect.

✳ Small premade royal icing decorations in myriad shapes, from flowers to basketballs to rubber duckies, are cute on cutout cookie shapes for certain occasions and are a quick way to give cookies a professional look.

To buy any of these decorating supplies, see Resources page, 216.

Gingerbread
Men

This little guy wears a traditional three-button suit, but feel free to dress him up as you wish.

These fragrant, spicy, buttery gingerbread men are meant to be eaten. If your fellas are destined to be tree decorations, however, you'll want to substitute ½ cup of vegetable shortening for the butter, which will give them a longer shelf life (several weeks). And don't forget to make a hole at the top of the cookie before baking through which to thread a piece of ribbon or yarn. Although gingerbread men usually strut their stuff at Christmastime, don't be afraid to break them out earlier in the year. "Dressed" creatively—think tuxedo for a wedding shower, bathing suit for Memorial Day—they're welcome guests at cookie swaps year-round.

MAKES: 60 three-inch or 24 six-inch cookies
BAKE TIME: 8 to 12 minutes
FREEZE ME!

½ cup (1 stick) unsalted butter, at room temperature

½ cup sugar

1 teaspoon baking powder

1 teaspoon ground ginger

½ teaspoon baking soda

½ teaspoon salt

½ teaspoon ground cinnamon

¼ teaspoon ground cloves

½ cup dark (not light or blackstrap) molasses

1 large egg

1 tablespoon distilled white vinegar

2½ cups unbleached all-purpose flour, plus extra for rolling the dough

Chocolate chips, cinnamon Red Hots, raisins, for eyes and buttons (optional)

Royal Icing (page 139), for decorating (optional)

>> **A STEP AHEAD**

Wrap the dough in plastic, place it in a zipper-lock plastic freezer bag, and store it in the freezer for up to 1 month. Defrost the dough in the refrigerator overnight, then let it stand on the countertop for 15 minutes to soften before proceeding with the recipe from Step 3.

1. Place the butter and sugar in a large bowl and beat together with an electric mixer on medium-high until well combined, 2 to 3 minutes. Add the baking powder, ginger, baking soda, salt, cinnamon, and cloves, and beat until incorporated. Add the molasses, egg, and vinegar and beat until smooth, scraping down the sides of the bowl once or twice as necessary. Stir in the flour, 1 cup at a time, until incorporated.

2. Scrape the dough onto a sheet of plastic wrap and press it into a rough square. Wrap it tightly and refrigerate it for at least 3 hours or up to 3 days. (The dough can be frozen at this point; see "A Step Ahead," left.)

3. Preheat the oven to 375°F. Line several baking sheets with parchment paper.

4. On a lightly floured work surface, using a lightly floured rolling pin, roll out the dough to a thickness of ¼ inch. Use a 3- or 6-inch gingerbread man cookie cutter to cut the dough, rerolling and cutting the scraps. Place the cut cookies on the prepared baking sheets. Make eyes, nose, mouth, and buttons by pressing chocolate chips, Red Hots, and/or raisins, into the cookies (alternatively, you can add these features to the baked cookies using Royal Icing). Cut out a hole at the top of each cookie with a drinking straw if desired.

5. Bake the cookies until they are firm, 8 to 12 minutes (smaller cookies will take less time than larger ones). Slide the parchment sheets with the cookies onto a wire rack and let the cookies cool completely.

6. Decorate the cooled cookies with Royal Icing, if desired, and let stand until the icing sets up, 30 minutes. If using the cookies as ornaments, thread a 6-inch length of ribbon through the hole of each one and knot it.

Gingerbread Men will keep, layered between parchment paper, in an airtight container at room temperature for up to 1 week (when made with butter) or for several weeks (when made with vegetable shortening).

And the Award Goes to . . . // OSCAR NIGHT COOKIE SWAP

Why not combine Oscar viewing with a cookie swap? As the host, set the theme by making gingerbread Oscar statuettes (for a cutter, go to www.cheapcookiecutters.com). Ask your guests to bring elegant black tie treats such as Cardamom Palmiers (page 86), Pistachio Sacristans (page 83), Fig and Fennel Biscotti (page 156), and Cayenne-Dusted Cheddar Coins (page 183). Invite people over early, so you can swap during the red carpet portion of the show. Buy Movie Reel cookie tins from e-cookietins.com for guests to pack up their cookies. Set up fruit and cheese platters, put some champagne or sparkling wine on ice, and let people help themselves before settling down to watch who wins.

Rolled Chocolate Cookies

with Simple Chocolate Icing

With black royal icing on its wings and black sanding sugar on its chocolate-iced body, this bat is eerily realistic.

MAKES: 48 two-inch or 24 four-inch cookies

BAKE TIME: 8 minutes

FREEZE ME!

This is the perfect dough to use for spooky Halloween cookies such as bats, cats, and witches. It bakes up dark and has a rich chocolate flavor. I also love to use it for other cookie shapes—especially poodles (in honor of our beloved dog, Mila). The Simple Chocolate Icing gives these cookies an extra chocolate kick, but you can frost them with Royal Icing or a combination, if you prefer.

1¾ cups unbleached all-purpose flour, plus extra for rolling the dough

½ cup unsweetened cocoa powder (natural or Dutch-process)

¼ teaspoon salt

1 cup (2 sticks) unsalted butter, at room temperature

½ cup sugar

1 large egg yolk

1 teaspoon pure vanilla extract

Simple Chocolate Icing (recipe follows) and/or Royal Icing (page 139), for decorating

Black sanding sugar, for decorating (optional)

1. Whisk together the flour, cocoa powder, and salt in a medium bowl.

2. Place the butter and sugar in a large bowl and beat together with an electric mixer on medium-high until fluffy, 2 to 3 minutes. Add the egg yolk and vanilla and beat until incorporated, scraping down the sides of the bowl as necessary. Add the flour mixture, a little at a time, beating on low until the dough comes together in a ball.

3. Divide the dough into 3 equal balls. Wrap each ball in plastic and refrigerate them for at least 2 hours or for up to 2 days. (The dough may be frozen at this point; see "A Step Ahead," right.)

4. Preheat the oven to 375°F. Line several baking sheets with parchment paper.

5. Remove one ball from the refrigerator and knead it 4 or 5 times on a lightly floured work surface to soften it. With a lightly floured rolling pin, roll out the dough to a thickness of ⅛ inch. Cut it into the desired shapes and place the cookies on the prepared baking sheets. Knead together the scraps, wrap them in plastic, and refrigerate them.

6. Bake the cookies until they are firm and dry, about 8 minutes. Slide the parchment sheets with the cookies onto wire racks and let the cookies cool completely.

7. Repeat Steps 5 and 6, using fresh parchment paper, with the remaining balls of dough and the scraps.

8. When the cookies are cool, use a small offset spatula to spread a thin layer of icing over each one. Let the iced cookies stand until the icing has hardened, about 30 minutes.

Rolled Chocolate Cookies will keep, layered between parchment paper, in an airtight container at room temperature for up to 5 days.

>> **A STEP AHEAD**

The dough can be wrapped in a double layer of plastic and then a layer of heavy-duty foil and frozen for up to 1 month. Defrost it in the refrigerator for at least 5 hours or overnight before proceeding as directed from Step 4.

Create cobwebs by frosting the cookies with white icing, piping a black spiral on top, and drawing the tip of a toothpick in lines from the center of the cookie toward the edge.

Simple Chocolate Icing

MAKES: enough to decorate 48 small or 24 large rolled cookies

A dd just a small amount of cocoa powder to the standard Royal Icing recipe (page 139) and you'll get a smooth, shiny icing with mild chocolate flavor and a pretty milk chocolate color.

2 tablespoons meringue powder (see Note)

5 tablespoons warm water

2 cups confectioners' sugar

2 tablespoons unsweetened cocoa powder (preferably natural, but Dutch-process will work)

1. Combine the meringue powder and water in a medium bowl. With an electric mixer fitted with the whisk attachment, beat the mixture on high until soft peaks form, 1 to 2 minutes. Add the confectioners' sugar and cocoa powder and beat until the icing is shiny and smooth, 3 to 5 minutes.

2. Use immediately, or press plastic onto the surface of the icing (otherwise the icing will begin to harden) and refrigerate it until you are ready to use it, for up to 1 day. Spread the icing on the cooled cookies with a small offset spatula or craft stick, and/or place it in a pastry bag fitted with a small, plain tip (or a ziplock bag with a small hole snipped in one corner). Pipe the icing decoratively onto the cookies. Let iced cookies stand until the icing sets up, 30 minutes.

Note: Meringue powder is available at Williams-Sonoma stores, and also from King Arthur Flour (www .kingarthurflour.com). Dried egg whites will work in a pinch, but meringue powder is preferred.

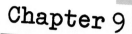

SLAM DUNK

BISCOTTI AND MANDELBROT

It may be hard to believe, but our favorite Italian-style cookies, bursting with luxury ingredients like chocolate, nuts, and dried fruit, sprang from utilitarian origins. Biscotti were originally conceived of as a long-keeping food for Italian travelers. They were carried and consumed by the Roman legions, and that wise man Pliny the Elder remarked they would still be edible many years after being baked. While I wouldn't exactly follow Pliny's example, he was obviously on to something: One of the appeals of this type of cookie—and its Jewish sister, Mandelbrot—is its long shelf life. Biscotti made without butter will keep for up to three weeks, and even biscotti containing some butter will keep for a week. For cookie swappers, this means you have considerable flexibility in timing your kitchen work.

Biscotti and Mandelbrot dough is shaped into long flat logs, baked, and then sliced into individual cookies. The cookies are then returned to the oven (biscotti means "twice baked" in Italian) to crisp up and dry out. Here are a few tips for dunkable-cookie baking:

* **Coarsely chop any nuts** before you stir them into the dough. It is easier to slice cleanly through the baked logs if the nuts are broken up.

* **If you'd like, you can score the dough logs,** cutting about one-third of the way through, with a serrated knife, before baking. This will make slicing easier once the logs have cooled.

* **Brush your dough logs** with beaten egg before baking. Even the plainest biscotti are beautified by the sheen of an egg wash (aren't we all?).

* **Resist the temptation to slice the logs** while they are still warm. They may crumble if not allowed to cool and firm up.

* **Decide how crunchy you want your biscotti to be,** and then adjust the second baking time accordingly. If you plan on dunking your cookies, bake them longer, so they'll dry out thoroughly, enabling them to absorb wine, coffee, or milk. If you are going to eat them straight from the cookie jar, shave a few minutes off of that final baking time, so they'll be crisp but not rock-hard.

Perfect for dunking, crunching, and swapping.

Classic
Almond Biscotti

This is a recipe my husband learned as a cooking student in Florence twenty-five years ago. We've been making it, with many variations, ever since. The biscotti are stuffed with almonds and are golden yellow from the eggs and egg yolks that moisten the batter (traditional biscotti like these don't have any butter).

Italians bake their biscotti until they are quite hard, with the intention of softening them up by dipping them in sweet wine, coffee, or tea. If you don't think your friends will be dipping the cookies, adjust the second baking time downward (to about 9 minutes), which will give the cookies a more tender, yielding texture.

MAKES: 48 biscotti
BAKE TIME:
44 to 47 minutes
FREEZE ME!

¾ cup whole almonds

2 cups unbleached all-purpose flour, plus extra for working the dough

1 cup sugar

½ teaspoon baking powder

¼ teaspoon salt

2 large egg yolks

3 large eggs

1 teaspoon pure vanilla extract

1. Preheat the oven to 350°F.

2. Spread the almonds on a large baking sheet and toast them until fragrant, watching them carefully to be sure they don't burn, 6 to 8 minutes. Set them aside to cool. When they are cool, coarsely chop them. Line another large baking sheet with parchment paper.

A STEP AHEAD

The dough logs can be wrapped in a double layer of plastic and a layer of heavy-duty foil and frozen for up to 1 month. Defrost in the refrigerator overnight before placing on a parchment-lined baking sheet and proceeding from Step 5.

3. Combine the flour, sugar, baking powder, and salt in a large bowl. Add the egg yolks, 2 of the whole eggs, and the vanilla and beat together with an electric mixer on low until just combined. Mix in the almonds.

4. Turn the dough out onto a lightly floured work surface and divide it in half. Shape each half into a flattened log about 16 inches long and 2½ inches wide. (The dough can be frozen at this point; see "A Step Ahead," left.) Place the logs several inches apart on the prepared baking sheet.

5. Place the remaining whole egg in a small bowl, beat it, and brush it over the dough. Bake the logs until they are firm to the touch, about 35 minutes. Remove the baking sheet from the oven to a wire rack and let the logs cool completely.

6. Reduce the oven temperature to 325°F. Transfer the logs to a cutting board and cut them widthwise into ¾-inch-thick slices. Lay the slices cut side down on the parchment-lined baking sheet.

7. Bake the cookies until they are crisp, 9 to 12 minutes. Transfer the cookies to wire racks and let them cool completely.

Classic Almond Biscotti will keep in an airtight container at room temperature for 2 to 3 weeks.

HOW SWEET IT IS :: COOKIE-SCENTED PARTY FAVORS

Cookies in the morning, cookies in the evening, cookies at suppertime ... Now that there are so many cookie-scented products on the market, you can have cookies all day, every day—guilt free. Cookie "stuff" like candles, soap, and lip gloss make for sweet cookie party prizes and gifts. You can find candles in all sorts of delicious flavors, including biscotti, hot fudge brownie, oatmeal raisin, snickerdoodle, and chocolate chip. Little soaps in the shape of Oreos and fortune cookies are also adorable. One of my favorite party favors, Powdered Sugar Cookie lip gloss from Philosophy, is a bit on the pricey side (typically twelve dollars; available at Sephora, department stores, and online at www.philosophy.com), but it's so yummy it may just be worth the extra (*ahem*) dough. (For more information, see Resources, page 216.)

Blueberry-Almond Biscotti

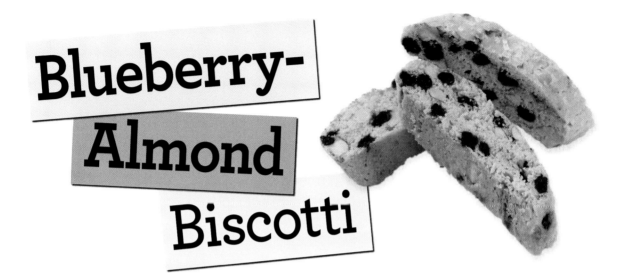

Dried blueberries add flavor, color, and texture to toothsome almond biscotti. Sprinkling some coarse white sanding sugar over the dough logs before the initial baking gives the cookies a glittering crust.

MAKES: 48 biscotti
BAKE TIME:
44 to 47 minutes
FREEZE ME!

¾ cup whole almonds

2 cups unbleached all-purpose flour, plus extra for working the dough

1 cup sugar

½ teaspoon baking powder

¼ teaspoon salt

3 large eggs

2 large egg yolks

½ teaspoon pure almond extract

¾ cup dried blueberries (see Note)

¼ cup coarse white sanding sugar (optional; see Resources, page 216)

1. Preheat the oven to 350°F.

2. Spread the almonds on a large baking sheet and toast them until fragrant, watching them carefully to be sure they don't burn, 6 to 8 minutes. Set them aside to cool. When they are cool, coarsely chop them. Line another large baking sheet with parchment paper.

3. Combine the flour, sugar, baking powder, and salt in a large bowl. Add 2 of the whole eggs, the egg yolks, and

›› A STEP AHEAD

The dough logs can be wrapped in a double layer of plastic and a layer of heavy-duty foil and frozen for up to 1 month. Defrost in the refrigerator overnight before placing on a parchment-lined baking sheet and proceeding from Step 5.

almond extract and beat together with an electric mixer on low until just combined. Beat in the almonds and blueberries on low.

4. Turn the dough out onto a lightly floured work surface and divide it in half. Shape each half into a flattened log about 16 inches long and 2½ inches wide. (The dough can be frozen at this point; see "A Step Ahead," left.) Place the logs several inches apart on the prepared baking sheet.

5. Place the remaining whole egg in a small bowl, beat it, and brush it over the dough. Sprinkle the dough with the sanding sugar if desired. Bake the logs until they are firm to the touch, about 35 minutes. Remove the baking sheet from the oven to a wire rack and let the logs cool completely.

6. Reduce the oven temperature to 325°F. Transfer the logs to a cutting board and cut them into ¾-inch-thick slices. Lay the slices cut side down on the parchment-lined baking sheet.

7. Bake the cookies until they are crisp, 9 to 12 minutes. Transfer the cookies to wire racks and let them cool completely.

Blueberry-Almond Biscotti will keep in an airtight container at room temperature for 1 to 2 weeks.

Note: Dried blueberries can be found in supermarkets where the other dried fruits, such as cranberries (Craisins), apricots, and prunes, are sold. You can also find them at gourmet markets.

VARIATION
Cranberry-Pistachio Biscotti
Substitute dried cranberries (Craisins) for the blueberries and shelled unsalted pistachios (no need to toast them) for the almonds. Use 1 teaspoon of pure vanilla extract in place of the almond extract. Stir in 1 teaspoon of grated orange zest along with the vanilla.

COOKIES IN THE KEY OF C A LITTLE SWAP MUSIC

Silence might be golden, but no cookie swap is complete without a well-beaten song mix. Thanks to iTunes and other digital music services, it is cheap and simple to buy a collection of songs tailored specifically for your event. Bust out Irish folk songs for St. Patrick's Day, mariachi music for Cinco de Mayo, or good old Christmas carols for your holiday bash. Take a hint from the party's theme—for example, an iTunes search for "baby" could unearth interesting choices for your baby shower. But what if your party is all about the cookies? These tasty morsels might sweeten the air:

The Oak Ridge Boys: "Christmas Cookies"

Billie Holiday: "Sugar"

Coastline: "Sugar Cookies"

Count Basie: "Cookie"

Michael Franks: "When the Cookie Jar Is Empty"

Carol Duboc: "Brownies and Wine"

The Searchers: "Sugar and Spice"

Wise Guys: "Chocolate Chip Cookies"

Cookie Monster: "Gingerbread Man"; "C is for Cookie"

Lonnie Mack: "Oreo Cookie Blues"

Lisa Loeb: "The Cookie Jar Song"

Ashford & Simpson: "Cookies and Cake"

The Archies: "Sugar, Sugar"

Strawberry Shortcake: "The Cookie Song"

Dark Chocolate
Biscotti
with Pine Nuts

Rich pine nuts give these chewy biscotti a slight crunch.

MAKES: 36 biscotti
BAKE TIME:
44 to 47 minutes
FREEZE ME!

Because they contain butter and brown sugar, these biscotti are more chewy than crunchy. Use natural cocoa powder, which is darker and has a stronger chocolate flavor than Dutch-process. Pine nuts give these biscotti delicate flavor and a subtle texture, but you can substitute other chopped nuts, if you like (skinned hazelnuts would be great, as would unsalted peanuts). To evoke Italy, serve these with small cups of espresso or glasses of sambuca and crank *Pagliacci*.

2 cups unbleached all-purpose flour, plus extra for working the dough

½ cup unsweetened natural cocoa powder

¾ teaspoon baking soda

½ teaspoon baking powder

½ teaspoon salt

6 tablespoons unsalted butter, at room temperature

⅔ cup packed light brown sugar

2 large eggs

1 teaspoon pure vanilla extract

1½ cups pine nuts

1. Preheat the oven to 350°F. Line a baking sheet with parchment paper.

2. Combine the flour, cocoa, baking soda, baking powder, and salt in a medium bowl.

3. Place the butter and sugar in a large bowl and beat together with an electric mixer on medium until fluffy, about 3 minutes. Add the eggs and the vanilla and beat until smooth. Beat in the flour mixture on low until just combined. Mix in the pine nuts.

4. Turn the dough out onto a lightly floured work surface and divide it in half. Shape each half into a flat log about 16 inches long and 2½ inches wide. Place the logs several inches apart on the prepared baking sheet. (The dough can be frozen at this point; see "A Step Ahead," right.)

5. Bake the logs until they are firm to the touch, about 35 minutes. Remove the baking sheet from the oven to a wire rack and let the logs cool completely.

6. Reduce the oven temperature to 325°F. Transfer the logs to a cutting board and cut them widthwise into ¾-inch-thick slices. Lay the slices cut side down on the parchment-lined baking sheet.

7. Bake the cookies until they are crisp, 9 to 12 minutes. Transfer the cookies to wire racks and let them cool completely.

Dark Chocolate Biscotti with Pine Nuts will keep an airtight container at room temperature in for up to 1 week.

>> **A STEP AHEAD**

The dough logs can be wrapped in a double layer of plastic and a layer of heavy-duty foil and frozen for up to 1 month. Defrost in the refrigerator overnight before placing on a parchment-lined baking sheet and proceeding as directed from Step 4.

PINING AWAY   A CONSUMER'S GUIDE TO PINE NUTS

Searching for more affordable pine nuts? Sorry to break the bad news, but the cost of these toothsome little morsels probably won't decrease anytime soon. Pine nuts are actually the seeds found in pinecones. The reason they are so expensive, compared to peanuts or walnuts, is that they have to be hand-harvested from wild, uncultivated trees, and it takes a pine tree fifteen to twenty-five years to begin producing the seeds.

If the cost of these tree nuts makes you quake like an aspen, go ahead and substitute something more economical, such as chopped almonds or walnuts.

Fig and Fennel Biscotti

Dense, chewy, and subtly licorice-y, these are wonderful at Christmastime.

MAKES: 36 biscotti

BAKE TIME: 44 to 47 minutes

FREEZE ME!

During the holidays I stuff dried figs with walnuts and fennel seeds. I found the recipe in a book by Italian food authority Faith Willinger and it is one of my favorite Christmas treats. The combination is unexpected and sublime. The walnuts add richness and a bit of crunch to the concentrated sweetness of the dried fruit, and the fennel seeds give the healthy bonbons an unexpected spiciness. These sophisticated biscotti were inspired by that sweetmeat. Willinger adds bay leaves to the container where she stores her figs. Try adding a bay leaf or two to your cookie container. When you unpack your biscotti for swapping they will be subtly and beautifully perfumed. Serve them with small glasses of sherry or another favorite fortified wine.

1⅓ cups walnuts

1¾ cups unbleached all-purpose flour, plus extra for working the dough

1 teaspoon fennel seeds (see Note)

¼ teaspoon baking powder

¼ teaspoon salt

5 tablespoons unsalted butter, at room temperature

½ cup light packed brown sugar

⅓ cup granulated sugar

2 large eggs

1 teaspoon pure vanilla extract

1 cup dried figs, tough stems removed, cut into ¼-inch pieces

1. Preheat the oven to 350°F.

2. Spread the walnuts on a large baking sheet and toast them until fragrant, watching them carefully to make sure they don't burn, 6 to 8 minutes. Set them aside to cool. When they are cool, coarsely chop them. Line another large baking sheet with parchment paper.

3. Combine the flour, fennel seeds, baking powder, and salt in a medium bowl.

Brideshead Revisited // BRIDAL SHOWER COOKIE SWAP

Some brides might not want to admit it, but showers can be a real snooze. If you balk at the idea of completing yet another wedding word search or fashioning yet another ribbon-and-bow bonnet, consider a swap your sweet relief. Cookie exchanges make a lot of sense, shower-wise. They're perfectly appropriate for either a single-sex or coed party (after all, guys like cookies, too), and they allow you to keep costs down—and the party short—by keeping the food simple. Let's say you call the party for the afternoon, from two o'clock to five o'clock. Instead of providing a full meal, you can think snacks such as cheese trays, fresh fruit, crudités and dip, olives, and nuts. Or you can have a casual barbecue, with hot dogs, hamburgers, potato salad, coleslaw, and plenty of beer (a menu that might appeal to husbands and boyfriends whose biggest fear about attending a shower is that there won't be enough food—or any "fun"). In either case, reserve some of the cookies for dessert (consider a diamond-ring- or bride-and-groom-shaped cookie as your own contribution—CopperGifts has these and many other wedding-themed cookie cutters). Guests might arrive with baking gifts for the happy couple, such as cookie sheets, cake pans, and oven mitts. They'll leave the party with a delicious assortment of sweets. And if you're motivated and extra-nice, you can create a memory book for the guest(s) of honor with pictures and recipes from the special day (see Resources, page 216).

›› A STEP AHEAD

The dough logs can be wrapped in a double layer of plastic and a layer of heavy-duty foil and frozen for up to 1 month. Defrost in the refrigerator overnight before placing on a parchment-lined baking sheet and proceeding from Step 6.

4. Place the butter and sugars in a large bowl and beat together with an electric mixer on medium until fluffy, about 3 minutes. Add 1 egg and the vanilla and beat until smooth. Beat in the flour mixture on low until just combined. Mix in the walnuts and figs.

5. Turn the dough out onto a lightly floured work surface and divide it in half. Shape each half into a flattened log about 16 inches long and 2½ inches wide. Place the logs several inches apart on the prepared baking sheet. (The dough can be frozen at this point; see "A Step Ahead," left.)

6. Beat the remaining egg and brush it over the dough. Bake the logs until they are firm to the touch, about 35 minutes. Remove the baking sheet from the oven to a wire rack and let the logs cool completely.

7. Reduce the oven temperature to 325°F. Transfer the logs to a cutting board and cut them widthwise into ¾-inch-thick slices. Lay the slices cut side down on the parchment-lined baking sheet.

8. Bake the cookies until they are crisp, 9 to 12 minutes. Transfer the cookies to wire racks and let them cool completely.

Fig and Fennel Biscotti will keep in an airtight container at room temperature for 2 to 3 weeks.

Note: I leave the fennel seeds whole, but if you'd like to make them smaller, feel free to crush them. Simply place them on a work surface and gently roll over them with a rolling pin.

Chocolate-Walnut Mandelbrot

Mandelbrot are twice-baked cookies similar to Italian biscotti. They're traditionally popular with Eastern European Jews, and because they're made with oil rather than butter they keep well, making them convenient for baking early in the week and serving on the Sabbath. Cookie swappers can take advantage of mandelbrot's long shelf life, baking them several days in advance of the party and knowing they'll stay fresh for days after they're exchanged. The combination of nuts, chocolate, and cinnamon is typical of some of the most beloved Eastern European treats, including rugelach and babka, which is why I chose it for this version of mandelbrot.

MAKES: 36 cookies
BAKE TIME: 40 to 45 minutes
FREEZE ME!

1¼ cups sugar

1 teaspoon ground cinnamon

2 cups unbleached all-purpose flour, plus extra for working the dough

½ cup unsweetened Dutch-process cocoa powder

2 teaspoons baking powder

¼ teaspoon ground cloves

½ teaspoon salt

5 large eggs

½ cup vegetable oil

1 teaspoon pure vanilla extract

1½ cup walnuts, coarsely chopped

1. Preheat the oven to 350°F. Line a baking sheet with parchment paper.

2. Combine ¼ cup of the sugar and the cinnamon in a shallow bowl and set it aside.

» A STEP AHEAD

The dough logs can be wrapped in a double layer of plastic and a layer of heavy-duty foil and frozen for up to 1 month. Defrost in the refrigerator overnight before placing on a parchment-lined baking sheet and proceeding from Step 6.

3. Whisk together the flour, cocoa powder, remaining 1 cup sugar, baking powder, cloves, and salt in a large bowl.

4. Place 4 of the eggs, the oil, and the vanilla in a medium bowl and whisk together until smooth. Add the egg mixture to the flour mixture and beat with an electric mixer on low until just combined. Mix in the walnuts.

5. Turn the dough out onto a lightly floured work surface and divide it in half. With floured hands (the dough will be sticky) shape each half into a flattened log about 16 inches long and 2½ inches wide. Place the logs several inches apart on the prepared baking sheet. (The dough can be frozen at this point; see "A Step Ahead," left.)

6. Lightly beat the remaining egg and brush it over the logs. Generously sprinkle the cinnamon sugar on top.

7. Bake the logs until they are lightly golden and have spread to about double in size, 25 to 30 minutes. Remove the baking sheet from the oven to a wire rack and let the logs cool completely.

8. Transfer the logs to a cutting board and cut them widthwise into ¾-inch-thick slices. Lay the slices cut side down on the baking sheet.

9. Bake the cookies until they are crisp, about 15 minutes. Transfer the cookies to wire racks and let them cool completely.

Chocolate-Walnut Mandelbrot will keep in an airtight container at room temperature for up to 1 week.

SAME BUT DIFFERENT :: BISCOTTI AND MANDELBROT

It's true: Both biscotti and mandelbrot are long, slender, crunchy cookies, just perfect for snacking and dunking. But traditionally, recipes for mandelbrot called for butter or oil, while recipes for biscotti did not. Added fat gave mandelbrot a more tender texture than biscotti, which were quite hard, on purpose. However, since biscotti caught on in such a big way back in the 1980s, bakers have been playing with the recipe, very often adding butter or oil for a more yielding cookie. So these days there is often very little difference between the two types of twice-baked cookies, except for the name.

Chapter 10

SOMETHING FOR EVERYONE

COOKIES FOR SPECIAL DIETS

ookie swaps are all about bringing people together, so you don't want to leave anyone out when it comes to the treats themselves. Everyone loves a good cookie, but not everyone can eat every cookie ingredient—some people are watching their sugar intake, some are avoiding wheat, still others are steering clear of added fat and cholesterol. So I've come up with some delectable cookies for swappers who want to contribute something that caters to these needs.

If you think that "low-fat" and "cookie" don't belong in the same sentence, you haven't tried meringue cookies, which are a simple mixture of egg whites whipped with sugar. With the addition of a few key ingredients, they become crowd-pleasing beauties. Raspberry Meringue Kisses get a surprising hit of flavor from raspberry Jell-O and mini chocolate chips (which you can omit, if you want to make non-fat cookies).

When I'm looking to limit sugar rather than fat, I make Sugar-Free Monkey Cookies. Sweetened with ripe bananas (which also moisten the batter) and naturally sweetened carob chips, these old-fashioned drop cookies don't contain any refined sugar but satisfy the sweet tooth nonetheless.

As wheat and gluten sensitivities and allergies become more widely diagnosed, a substantial number of people are limiting or altogether avoiding foods made with wheat or containing gluten. Some people have a mild sensitivity to either or both. Limiting wheat and gluten, by making wheat-free oatmeal-chocolate chip peanut butter cookies or low-gluten spelt brownies, is a way for some of these folks to have their cookies and eat them, too! (Of course, people who are truly allergic to either wheat or gluten should avoid any foods that contain these ingredients.)

As with all things, when baking for people with special dietary needs, common sense should be your guide. If you are making cookies for guests with food sensitivities or allergies of any kind, be sure to let them know exactly what your cookies contain, so they can decide for themselves whether to indulge or abstain.

Raspberry Meringue Kisses

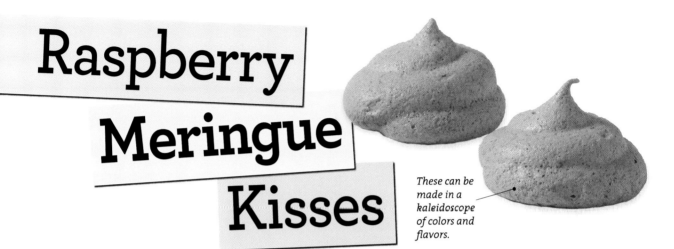

These can be made in a kaleidoscope of colors and flavors.

When it comes to low- or non-fat baking, I'd rather not employ tricks like substituting apple sauce for butter—the results never live up to my expectations. So when I'm seeking "healthier" sweets I turn to a recipe that, even when made by French pastry chefs, is traditionally low in fat: the meringue cookie. Made with not much more than egg whites and sugar, they are crispy and light.

The following recipe employs a packet of raspberry Jell-O, which gives the cookies a beautiful pink color and helps stabilize the whipped egg whites to keep the meringues as airy as possible. A small amount of mini chocolate chips makes these cookies a chocolate-and-raspberry delight, without adding much fat at all.

MAKES: 48 cookies
BAKE TIME: 30 to 40 minutes
QUICK PREP

3 large egg whites

⅛ teaspoon salt

1 package (3 ounces) raspberry Jell-O

½ cup sugar

1 teaspoon pure vanilla extract

1 cup mini chocolate chips (optional)

1. Position one oven rack in the top third of the oven and the other rack on the bottom third of the oven.

2. Preheat the oven to 275°F. Line 2 baking sheets with parchment paper.

3. Place the egg whites and salt in a large bowl and with an electric mixer fitted with the whisk attachment, beat on medium until they are frothy, about 30 seconds. Turn the speed to high and pour the Jell-O and then the sugar into the bowl in a slow, steady stream. Continue to beat until the egg whites are stiff and shiny, about 5 minutes.

4. Using a rubber spatula, gently fold in the vanilla and, if desired, the chocolate chips. Drop tablespoonfuls of the meringue onto the prepared baking sheets, leaving about 1½ inches between each cookie. (Alternatively, scrape the meringue into a pastry bag fitted with a very large plain or star tip and pipe the cookies, each about 1½ inches in diameter, onto the baking sheets.)

5. Bake the meringues until they are firm on the outside but still soft on the inside, about 30 minutes (for crispier meringues, bake them for 40 minutes). Slide the parchment sheet with the cookies to wire racks and let them cool for 5 minutes, then carefully peel them off the parchment paper.

Raspberry Meringue Kisses will keep in an airtight container at room temperature for 1 week.

VARIATIONS
A Rainbow of Meringue Cookies

Although most grown-ups will prefer the more sophisticated flavor combination of raspberry and chocolate, kids love meringues when they come in all sorts of flavors and colors. For a St. Patrick's Day swap, try lime gelatin (minus the chocolate chips). Orange is spooky fun for Halloween. Lemon yellow—or a bouquet of spring pastel colors—is wonderful for Easter. I can't think of an occasion where blueberry might work, but if you can, then go for it.

Go (No) Nuts! // THE NUT-FREE COOKIE SWAP

It goes without saying that nuts are crunchy, rich, and delicious, but they do cause serious and even deadly allergic reactions in some people. When organizing a swap, it's a good idea to ask your guests if they are allergic. Depending on how many people are affected and how serious their allergies are, you can decide how to proceed. It may be sufficient to identify which cookies have nuts, or you may want to throw an entirely nut-free swap.

If you'll be mixing nutty cookies with nut-free, give guests cards to ID their cookies and any potentially harmful ingredients. And then take an extra step: Avoid cross-contamination. Put all nut-free cookies on one table instead of commingling your goodies.

No-nut people are sensitive to the smell of allergens, and allergen dust on someone's hand can rub off on other finger foods, so be smart about your non-cookie noshes as well. Safe and tasty snacks include Nori-Maki snack mix, wasabi peas, and other Asian rice cracker mixes; honey wheat pretzels; Gerbs pumpkin seeds (www.gerbspumpkinseeds.com); and homemade nut-free trail mix.

When baking for and swapping with the nut allergic, READ THE LABEL of a) the food you serve and b) the ingredients you use in baking.

Although the FDA does not have helpful guidelines for processed foods, many chocolates and other ingredients may have a warning label. And luckily, some manufacturers are cottoning to the idea of safe baking products, such as Peanut Free Planet (www.peanutfreeplanet .com), Divvies (www.divvies.com), and Enjoy Life (www.enjoylifefoods.com). Even Hershey's is allergen-friendly and segregates during their processing (for more info, visit www.hersheys.com/ nutrition/allergens.asp)—again, read the label to make sure you have picked the right chocolate.

There are enough great recipes in this book to help you go nut-free with ease (or feel free to omit nuts from other recipes). Some suggestions to get you started:

* Very Vanilla Sprinkle Cookies (*page 49*)
* Incredibly Fudgy Brownies (*page 55*)
* Espresso Squares (*page 100*)
* Jam-Filled Lemon Sandwich Cookies (*page 111*)
* Flaky Pastry Pinwheels (*page 81*)
* Vanilla Pretzels (*page 132*)
* Gingerbread Men (*page 141*)
* Raspberry Meringue Kisses (*page 163*)

For more information on food allergies, including product recalls, visit the Food Allergy and Anaphylaxis Network (FAAN) at www.foodallergy.org.

Wheat-Free Oatmeal Cookies

with Chocolate Chips and Peanut Butter

MAKES:
48 cookies
BAKE TIME:
12 minutes
QUICK PREP
FREEZE ME!

These delicious cookies let wheat-sensitive people enjoy the classic cookie trifecta—chocolate chip, oatmeal, and peanut butter—in one scrumptious bite. But they are so stuffed with old-fashioned goodness that they'll be popular with everyone at your party. I think of them as small miracles: Despite the fact that they contain no flour, they have a very cookie-like texture.

3 cups rolled oats (not instant)

1½ teaspoons baking soda

½ teaspoon salt

1⅓ cups smooth peanut butter
(preferably commercial)

6 tablespoons unsalted butter,
at room temperature

⅔ cup granulated sugar

⅔ cup packed light brown sugar

2 large eggs

2 teaspoons pure vanilla extract

2 cups semisweet chocolate chips

1. Preheat the oven to 350°F. Line 2 baking sheets with parchment paper.

2. Combine the oats, baking soda, and salt in a medium bowl.

3. Place the peanut butter, butter, and sugars in a large mixing bowl and beat together with an electric mixer on medium-high until smooth, 2 to 3 minutes. Add the eggs and vanilla and beat until smooth. Beat in the oat mixture on low until just incorporated. Mix in the chocolate chips.

4. Drop the dough by heaping tablespoonfuls onto the prepared baking sheets, leaving about 3 inches between each cookie. (The dough can be frozen at this point; see "A Step Ahead," right.)

5. Bake the cookies until they are golden around the edges but still soft on top, about 12 minutes. Let the cookies stand on the baking sheets for 5 minutes, then carefully slide the parchment sheet with the cookies to a wire rack and let them cool completely.

Wheat-free Oatmeal Cookies with Chocolate Chips and Peanut Butter will keep in an airtight container at room temperature for 3 to 4 days.

>> **A STEP AHEAD**

The dropped dough can be frozen on the baking sheets, transferred to ziplock freezer bags, and stored in the freezer for up to 1 month. Transfer frozen dough to parchment-lined baking sheets and bake a minute or two longer than directed.

Spelt Flour Brownies

Dense and chewy, these are yummy and healthful (for a brownie, that is).

MAKES: 36 brownies
BAKE TIME:
25 to 30 minutes
FREEZE ME!

S pelt is an ancient grain related to wheat. It's packed with protein and nutrients but has a lower gluten content than wheat, making it more digestible for many people with mild gluten sensitivity (though not, unfortunately, for people with a gluten allergy; if your guests are allergic to gluten, then they will have to avoid wheat in all its forms, including spelt).

No problem with gluten? There are other reasons to try spelt. It is packed with more protein than wheat flour, and its tough husk means that it can be grown without pesticides, making it good for the environment as well as the body.

Nonstick cooking spray

1½ cups unsweetened Dutch-process cocoa powder

1 tablespoon instant espresso powder

1 cup spelt flour (see Note)

1 teaspoon baking powder

½ teaspoon salt

2 cups packed light brown sugar

4 large eggs

6 tablespoons unsalted butter, melted and cooled

2 teaspoons pure vanilla extract

1½ cups pitted prunes, finely chopped

1. Preheat the oven to 350°F. Line a 9-by-13-inch pan with heavy-duty aluminum foil, making sure the foil is tucked into all the corners and there is at least 1 inch overhanging the top of the pan on all sides. Spray the bottom and sides with nonstick cooking spray.

Spelling It Out BAKING COOKIES WITH SPELT FLOUR

It helps to know a little bit about the properties of spelt flour before deciding when and how to substitute it for wheat flour in a cookie recipe.

First, consider flavor. Spelt has a more assertive, nutty flavor than white flour, comparable to but not exactly like whole wheat flour. Think about the flavor impact spelt flour will have on your recipe before you swap it in. Will its nuttiness play up the other ingredients, or will it be a distraction? Spelt works well with rich and flavorful additions such as seeds, nuts, dried fruit, coffee, and chocolate, all of which can stand up to it, but it tends to overwhelm delicate vanilla cookies and other mildly flavored confections.

Second, think texture. Gluten is the web of protein strands that forms when flour is mixed with a liquid. It provides the structure that allows baked goods to rise high in the oven without falling. Because spelt doesn't develop nearly as much gluten as wheat flour, it won't provide as strong of a web. It is great in recipes like brownies, where a dense, soft texture is desirable. But in recipes where you want your cookies to rise and stay tall when they're cool (biscotti and rugelach are two examples), spelt isn't the best choice. Even when making spelt brownies you should take care not to overmix your dough, so as not to destroy the fragile strands of gluten that do develop.

Third, be forewarned that spelt flour doesn't absorb as much liquid as wheat flour. This isn't as much of an issue with cookies, which don't often call for significant quantities of milk the way cake recipes do. But if your cookie recipe does contain liquid, hold back a few tablespoons when adding it, adding the rest gradually and with discretion, to avoid an overly sticky or loose dough.

2. Sift together the cocoa powder, espresso powder, spelt flour, baking powder, and salt in a medium bowl.

3. Combine the sugar, eggs, butter, vanilla, and prunes in a food processor and pulse several times until almost smooth. Scrape the wet ingredients into the bowl containing the dry ingredients and stir until just moistened. Stir in the cocoa mixture until just incorporated (be careful not to overmix, which will break down the gluten in the batter and make the

Remove the cooled, uncut bars from the pan by grasping the overhanging foil and pulling it up. Peel away the foil and wrap the bars in a double layer of plastic and then a layer of heavy-duty foil. Freeze for up to 2 weeks. Defrost on the countertop for several hours before cutting into bars.

brownies tough). Pour the batter into the prepared pan.

4. Bake the brownies until they are just set in the center, 25 to 30 minutes. Let cool completely on a wire rack. (The brownies can be frozen at this point; see "A Step Ahead," left.)

5. Grasping the overhanging foil on either side of the pan, lift out the

brownies and place them on a cutting board. Cut the brownies into 32 squares and peel them from the foil.

Spelt Flour Brownies will keep at room temperature in an airtight container for up to 3 days.

Note: Spelt flour can be purchased at almost any natural foods supermarket.

Sugar-Free Monkey Cookies

These banana-flavored cookies will please all the little monkeys at your swap.

Bananas are front and center in this delightfully tender, slightly sweet, satisfying cookie. They lend their natural sweetness to the dough, so no refined sugar is required, and coconut and oats give the cookies an interesting, toothsome texture.

For the best result, let your bananas sit on the countertop until the skins are almost all brown; this signals when their sugars are completely developed. Look for carob chips sweetened with barley syrup at the natural foods store, or replace them with raisins if you prefer. You'll be surprised by how addictive these wholesome cookies are. Don't tell my kids I said so, but they're even good for breakfast!

MAKES:
60 cookies
BAKE TIME:
12 minutes
QUICK PREP
FREEZE ME!

1 cup unbleached all-purpose flour

⅔ cup shredded unsweetened coconut

2 teaspoons baking powder

1 teaspoon salt

2 cups mashed, very ripe bananas
   (about 4 large bananas)

½ cup (1 stick) unsalted butter,
   melted and cooled

2 large eggs

1 teaspoon pure vanilla extract

4 cups rolled oats (not instant)

1½ cups carob chips

» A STEP AHEAD

The dropped dough can be frozen on the baking sheets, transferred to ziplock plastic freezer bags, and stored in the freezer for up to 1 month. Frozen dough should be placed on parchment-lined baking sheets and defrosted for 10 minutes before flattening the cookies and proceeding as directed.

1. Preheat the oven to 350°F. Line several baking sheets with parchment paper.

2. Combine the flour, coconut, baking powder, and salt in a medium bowl.

3. Place the mashed bananas and butter in a large bowl and beat with an electric mixer on medium until smooth, 2 to 3 minutes. Add the eggs and vanilla and beat until smooth. Beat in the flour mixture on low. Stir in the oats and carob chips.

4. Drop the dough by heaping tablespoonfuls onto the prepared baking sheets, leaving about 3 inches between each cookie. Flatten each one slightly with the palm of your hand. (The dough can be frozen at this point; see "A Step Ahead," left.)

5. Bake the cookies until they are golden around the edges but still soft on top, about 12 minutes. Let the cookies stand on the baking sheets for 5 minutes, then carefully slide the parchment sheets with the cookies to wire racks and let them cool completely.

Sugar-Free Monkey Chip Cookies will keep in an airtight container at room temperature for 3 to 4 days.

Lean, Mean, Green // AN ECO-LOVERS SWAP

Tree huggers and cookie swappers unite! Throw an earth-conscious cookie swap to celebrate Earth Day on April 22 (or show Mom Earth you love her any time of year). Invite guests electronically using www.socializr.com (a user-friendlier alternative to Evite) or the exceedingly simple, if bare bones, www.invitastic.com. Suggest walking, biking, and carpooling as a means of transportation. Ask your guests to seek out organic ingredients to use, and serve them local, organic food and drink. Know a nearby eco-expert? Invite him or her as a guest speaker, or consider screening an inspiring or educational documentary (the *Planet Earth* series is stunning, and its enviro-message is very subtle). Decorate your table with potted seedlings, which can later be planted outside, or given as gifts. You might hang compact fluorescent lightbulbs as decoration and then ask guests to take one home with them, or provide paints, paintbrushes, and have everyone decorate a flowerpot. Other great party favors include reusable shopping bags for cookie transportation (www .chicobag.com), adorable travel mugs, water bottles, or lunch totes.

Alternatively, use the cookie swap as incentive to do green deeds in your community. Invite participants to a local river cleanup, tree or vegetable planting, recycling fair, or other hands-on project. Afterward, have a cookie swap picnic on a nearby grassy knoll to celebrate your hard work. The community service and physical activity might just convince your perpetually dieting friends to participate!

Chapter 11

SNACK ATTACK

SAVORY COOKIES

If "savory cookie" sounds like an oxymoron, try coming back to the idea after baking and eating batch after batch of the sweet kind. It will make perfect sense! One taste will make you a convert—you'll see that rich, buttery, bite-size cookies are just as appealing when they're flavored with cheese, olives, herbs, and sea salt as when they're bursting with chocolate chips, nuts, and raisins.

You'll find my favorites in this chapter. Tote them along when you want to provide savory contrast to the sweet cookies that will dominate the swap table. Everyone will enjoy tucking into a few Black Pepper and Parmesan Animal Crackers or Poppy Seed and Rye Rounds along with their brownies and gingerbread men.

If you are hosting, consider putting out an extra batch of savory cookies for your guests to munch on when they arrive. This way, no one will be on sugar overload before the swap begins. You can even build a party menu around these tempting crackerlike treats. Let your savory cookie lead the way when you're choosing the rest of your menu: A heaping tray of Almond and Olive Biscotti alongside a platter of colorful cold antipasti (pickled mushrooms, roasted peppers, bocconcini, prosciutto, salami) make a great party presentation. If you are going to bake Cayenne-Dusted Cheddar Coins, you might supplement them with Southwestern-flavored snacks such as spiced pepitas (pumpkin seeds), guacamole with crudités, and black bean quesadillas. Or serve Rosemary Pecan Sandies, which might suggest Southern hospitality. How about rounding out your menu with deviled eggs and celery sticks spread with Pimiento cheese?

Baking these delicious savories is no more difficult than making any other kind of cookie. In fact, the cookies in this chapter fall into three categories—biscotti, rolled cookies, and icebox cookies. This means that should you seek guidance on preparing a certain savory cookie, you can turn to the relevant chapter for advice.

Almond and Olive Biscotti

Salty, crunchy, and oh so good, serve or swap these at your next Italian-themed party.

MAKES:
48 biscotti
BAKE TIME:
10 minutes
FREEZE ME!

These nutty, olive-and-Parmesan-laced cookies are absolutely phenomenal served with sliced sopressata and chilled pinot grigio. Cornmeal gives them a sunny color and pleasant crunch. Make up a batch to impress guests at a pre-swap cocktail hour, and then make some more for the exchange itself.

1 cup whole almonds

1½ cups unbleached all-purpose flour, plus extra for working the dough

½ cup finely ground yellow cornmeal, preferably stone-ground

2 teaspoons sugar

½ teaspoon baking powder

1 teaspoon salt

4 tablespoons (½ stick) unsalted butter, at room temperature

1 cup finely grated Parmesan cheese (about 2 ounces)

3 large eggs

¾ cup pitted green olives, chopped

2 teaspoons finely chopped fresh sage leaves

1. Preheat the oven to 350°F.

2. Spread the almonds on a large baking sheet and toast them until

fragrant, watching them carefully to be sure they don't burn, 6 to 8 minutes. Set them aside to cool. When they are cool, coarsely chop them. Line another large baking sheet with parchment paper.

3. Place the flour, cornmeal, sugar, baking powder, and salt in a large bowl and stir to combine. Add the butter and Parmesan and beat with an electric mixer on low until the mixture resembles coarse meal. Add the eggs and continue to beat until the dough comes together in a ball. Mix in the almonds, olives, and sage.

4. Turn the dough out onto a lightly floured work surface and divide it in half. Shape each half into a flattened log about 12 inches long and 2 inches wide. Place the logs several inches apart on the prepared baking sheet. (The dough logs can be frozen at this point; see "A Step Ahead," right.)

5. Bake the logs until they are firm to the touch, about 30 minutes. Remove the baking sheet from the oven to a wire rack and let the logs cool completely.

6. Reduce the oven temperature to 325°F. Transfer the logs to a cutting board and cut them into ½-inch-thick slices. Lay the slices cut side down on the parchment-lined baking sheet.

7. Bake the cookies until they are crisp, about 10 minutes. Transfer the cookies to wire racks and let them cool completely.

Almond and Olive Biscotti will keep in an airtight container at room temperature for 1 week.

VARIATION

Almond-Prosciutto-Parmesan Biscotti

At the deli counter, ask for a ¼-pound piece of prosciutto cut into a ¼-inch thick slab. Chop the prosciutto into ¼-inch dice and add it in place of the olives.

>> **A STEP AHEAD**

The dough logs can be wrapped in a double layer of plastic and a layer of heavy-duty foil and frozen for up to 1 month. Defrost in the refrigerator overnight before placing on a parchment-lined baking sheet and proceeding from Step 5.

Black Pepper and Parmesan Animal Crackers

Thanks to the addition of black pepper, these little animals have some bite!

MAKES:
48 two-inch cookies
BAKE TIME: 8 minutes
FREEZE ME!

When it comes to this mildly peppery dough, any shape will do (hearts, spades, diamonds, and clubs are perfect for poker night), but I love to make animal crackers—the shapes add just a bit of cheekiness to an otherwise grown-up cracker. Bread flour makes these crisp and sturdy, perfect for dunking into cups of soup. If you prefer a more tender, crumbly cracker, you can use all-purpose flour instead.

2 cups bread flour, plus extra for working the dough

1 tablespoon freshly ground black pepper

1 teaspoon salt

1 cup finely grated Parmesan cheese (about 2 ounces)

12 tablespoons (1½ sticks) unsalted butter, chilled, cut into small pieces

1 tablespoon milk, plus a teaspoon or two more if necessary

1. Place the flour, pepper, and salt in a food processor and pulse to combine. Add the cheese, butter, and 1 tablespoon milk, and pulse until the mixture resembles coarse meal (do not overprocess).

2. Knead the dough in the bowl slightly, just until it comes together, adding the extra milk as necessary.

3. Turn the dough out onto a lightly floured work surface and shape it into a 6-inch disk. Wrap it in plastic and refrigerate it for at least 2 hours or for up to 2 days. (the dough can be frozen at this point, see "A Step Ahead," right.)

4. Preheat the oven to 375°F. Line several baking sheets with parchment paper.

5. Remove the dough disk from the refrigerator and knead it 4 to 5 times on a lightly floured work surface to soften it. With a lightly floured rolling pin, roll out the dough to a thickness of ⅛ inch. Use 2-inch animal-shaped cookie cutters (or any other shapes) to cut cookies, placing them about 1 inch apart on the prepared baking sheets. Combine, wrap, and refrigerate the scraps.

6. Bake the cookies until they are firm and golden around the edges, about 8 minutes. Slide the parchment sheets with the cookies onto a wire rack and let the cookies cool completely.

7. Roll, cut, and bake the scraps as directed in Steps 5 and 6, using fresh parchment paper.

Black Pepper and Parmesan Animal Crackers will keep in an airtight container at room temperature for 3 to 4 days.

>> **A STEP AHEAD**

The dough disk can be wrapped in a double layer of plastic and then a layer of heavy-duty foil and frozen for up to 1 month. Defrost for at least 5 hours or overnight before proceeding as directed from Step 4.

Hodgepodge // A CACOPHONY OF COOKIE SWAP CONCEPTS

Bust out of a seasonal swap rut with some out-of-the-box exchange ideas:

* **Around the World Cookie Swap:** Make it multicultural with cookies or snacks from different countries or regions. Assign an area to each guest.

* **Doggie Biscuit Cookie Swap:** Invite over chums from your dog park or doggie day care to swap human cookies and/or biscuits for your four-legged friends.

* **Dough Swap:** Swap frozen dough in cartons—labeled with baking directions of course!—ready to be whipped out of the freezer at a moment's notice. (You might want to bake up a few samples of the dough first to give people a sneak peek.)

* **Empty Nesters' Swap:** Got the blues because your little babies have grown up and flown away? On the next Mother's or Father's Day, take comfort in the company of other parents with a cookie swap specifically for wistful mommy or daddy birds.

* **Gift Wrap Cookie Swap:** Is everyone balking at the idea of a holiday swap, referencing their ever-growing task list? Make it a productive night of cookie swapping *and* gift wrapping, complete with pretty ribbons and lavish wrapping paper.

* **Follow Your Bliss:** Center your swap around something that sparks your passion, like a beloved movie or important sporting event (the Super Bowl or Kentucky Derby are good choices) or the finale of your favorite TV series.

Poppy Seed and Rye Rounds

Rye flour gives these savories an earthy flavor, while cream cheese gives them a melt-in-your-mouth texture. They're very good on their own, but can also be used to make simple canapés: Top each one with a dab of crème fraîche and a small piece of smoked salmon. Now that I think of it, you may want to hold onto these instead of swapping them! Enjoy them with champagne or prosecco and make sure there's a plushly upholstered divan nearby—you'll swoon.

MAKES:
48 two-inch cookies
BAKE TIME:
12 to 15 minutes
FREEZE ME!

1 cup rye flour (see Note)

1 cup unbleached all-purpose flour, plus extra for working the dough

1 teaspoon salt

½ cup (1 stick) unsalted butter, at room temperature

½ package (4 ounces) cream cheese, at room temperature

2 tablespoons poppy seeds

1. Combine the rye flour, all-purpose flour, and salt in a food processor and pulse to combine. Add the butter and cream cheese and pulse until the mixture resembles coarse meal (do not overprocess).

2. Turn the mixture out onto a lightly floured work surface and shape the dough into a 6-inch disk. Wrap it in

>> **A STEP AHEAD**
The dough disk can be wrapped in a double layer of plastic and then a layer of heavy-duty foil and frozen for up to 1 month. Defrost in for at least 5 hours or overnight before proceeding as directed from Step 3.

plastic and refrigerate it for at least 2 hours or for up to 2 days. (The dough can be frozen at this point; see "A Step Ahead," left.)

3. Preheat the oven to 350°F. Line several baking sheets with parchment paper. Place the poppy seeds in a small, shallow bowl or dish.

4. Remove the dough disk from the refrigerator and knead it 4 to 5 times on a lightly floured work surface to soften it. With a lightly floured rolling pin, roll out the dough to a thickness of ¼ inch. Use a 2-inch round fluted cookie cutter (or any other desired shape) to cut cookies. Combine, wrap, and refrigerate the scraps.

5. Gently press one side of each cookie into the poppy seeds and then place it, seeded side up, on the prepared baking sheets.

6. Bake the cookies until they are firm and just coloring around the edges, 12 to 15 minutes. Slide the parchment sheets with the cookies onto a wire rack and let the cookies cool completely.

7. Roll, cut, and bake the scraps as directed in Steps 4 and 5, using fresh parchment paper.

Poppy Seed and Rye Rounds will keep, layered between parchment paper, in an airtight container at room temperature for 3 to 4 days.

Note: You can find rye flour at your natural foods store, as well as in the baking aisle of most supermarkets.

Cayenne-Dusted Cheddar Coins

Spicy and decadent, these luscious crackers are addictive. You've been warned!

Icebox cheese biscuits are among my favorite savory cookies, because of their luxurious richness and because they are deceptively easy to make. Use extra-sharp aged Cheddar cheese to intensify the flavor. For a milder cookie, you can substitute chili powder for the cayenne.

MAKES: 48 cookies
BAKE TIME: 13 to 15 minutes
FREEZE ME!

1 cup unbleached all-purpose flour

1 teaspoon salt

¼ teaspoon ground cumin

⅛ teaspoon ground coriander

½ cup (1 stick) unsalted butter, at room temperature

8 ounces extra-sharp aged Cheddar cheese, grated (about 2 cups)

1 large egg yolk

¾ teaspoon cayenne pepper

1. Combine the flour, salt, cumin, and coriander in a medium mixing bowl.

2. Place the butter, cheese, and egg yolk in a large bowl and beat with an electric mixer on medium-high, scraping down the sides of the bowl occasionally, until well combined, 2 to 3 minutes. Stir in the flour mixture until just incorporated.

>> **A STEP AHEAD**
The dough logs can be wrapped in a double layer of plastic and then a layer of heavy-duty foil and frozen for up to 1 month. Defrost them for at least 5 hours or overnight in the refrigerator before proceeding as directed from Step 4.

3. Divide the dough into two portions. Turn one portion out onto a piece of wax paper and shape it, rolling it inside the paper, into a log about 8 inches long and 1 inch in diameter. Wrap the log in plastic and refrigerate it for at least 2 hours (or for up to 24 hours). Repeat with the remaining dough. (The dough can be frozen at this point; see "A Step Ahead," left.)

4. Preheat the oven to 350°F. Line several baking sheets with parchment paper.

5. Remove the dough logs from the refrigerator and slice them into ⅓-inch-thick rounds.

6. Place the cookies at least 1 inch apart on the prepared baking sheets. Use a small strainer to sift some of the cayenne pepper over each cookie.

7. Bake the cookies until they are lightly golden around the edges but still soft on top, 13 to 15 minutes. Let them stand on the baking sheets for 5 minutes and then slide the parchment with the cookies onto a wire rack to cool completely.

Cayenne-Dusted Cheddar Coins will keep in an airtight container at room temperature for 3 to 4 days.

A sea salt garnish gives these sandies a surprising crunch.

Savory Rosemary Pecan Sandies

Here is a savory version of the classic lunch box favorite, with a little fresh rosemary thrown in. Like their sweet sisters, these cookies are crumbly, buttery, and studded with shards of rich pecans—but of course they're a bit salty, and the rosemary adds a fresh and slightly woodsy flavor and aroma. A touch of sea salt sprinkled on top of each cookie makes a minimalist garnish, but a couple of fresh rosemary leaves pressed on top would also be pretty.

MAKES:
about 48 cookies
BAKE TIME:
15 to 17 minutes
QUICK PREP
FREEZE ME!

1½ cups pecans

¾ cup (1½ sticks) **unsalted butter,
at room temperature**

1 tablespoon dark brown sugar

1½ teaspoons finely chopped fresh
rosemary

1 large egg yolk

1½ cups unbleached all-purpose flour

1½ teaspoons salt

Moderately coarse sea salt
(Maldon flakes are ideal), for garnish
(optional)

1. Place the pecans in a food processor and pulse 5 to 8 times until finely chopped (they should resemble very coarse sand).

2. Place the butter, brown sugar, and rosemary in a large bowl and beat together with an electric mixer on medium-high until fluffy, 2 to 3 minutes. Add the egg yolk and beat until smooth. Beat in the flour and salt on low until just incorporated. Beat in the chopped nuts.

» A STEP AHEAD

» A STEP AHEAD

The dough logs may be wrapped in a double layer of plastic and then a layer of heavy-duty foil and frozen for up to 1 month. Defrost them in the refrigerator for at least 5 hours or overnight before proceeding as directed from Step 4.

3. Divide the dough into two portions. Turn one portion out onto a piece of wax paper and shape it, rolling it inside the paper, into a log about 8 inches long and 2 inches in diameter. Wrap the dough in plastic and refrigerate it for at least 2 hours (or for up to 24 hours). Repeat with the remaining dough. (The dough can be frozen at this point; see "A Step Ahead," left.)

4. Preheat the oven to 350°F.

5. Remove the dough logs from the refrigerator and let them stand on the countertop to soften slightly, about 10 minutes. Slice the logs into ⅓-inch-thick rounds, rotating the dough often so it doesn't become misshapen as you cut it.

6. Place the cookies at least 2 inches apart on ungreased baking sheets. Sprinkle each one with a little bit of sea salt if desired.

7. Bake the cookies until they are lightly golden around the edges but still soft on top, 15 to 17 minutes. Let them stand on the baking sheet for 5 minutes and then remove them with a metal spatula to a wire rack to cool completely.

Savory Rosemary Pecan Sandies will keep in an airtight container at room temperature for 3 to 4 days.

VARIATIONS
Herb and Nut Shortbread Buttons

You may substitute any herb and nut combination that you like for the rosemary and pecans, with great results. Some combos to try: 2 teaspoons of chopped, fresh thyme leaves with toasted and skinned hazelnuts; 1 tablespoon of chopped, fresh parsley with almonds (I like to add ½ teaspoon of grated lemon zest to this dough); 1 tablespoon of chopped, fresh basil with toasted pine nuts. Feel free to play around with other pairings—let your taste and imagination guide you.

Sweet Pecan Sandies

To make traditional sweet pecan sandies, adjust the ingredient list as follows: Omit the dark brown sugar and use ½ cup firmly packed light brown sugar and ¼ cup confectioners' sugar instead. Omit the rosemary. Cut the salt to ¼ teaspoon and omit the coarse sea salt garnish. That's it! Enjoy.

Chapter 12

EASY PEASY

SHORTCUT COOKIES

I'm no stranger to baking batch upon batch of cookies, and then painstakingly decorating each one with piped icing and various gewgaws. But show me a shortcut cookie recipe—one that requires little or no baking at all—and I'm all for it! In fact, the first cookbook I wrote was a collection of recipes that didn't require any cooking. The second was for people whose only kitchen skill was the ability to bring water to a boil. I've written three books about icebox desserts, with recipes whose main ingredients include Nabisco Chocolate Wafers, Devil Dogs, and Twinkies. So it was an exciting challenge to come up

with this assortment of truly delicious, impossibly easy cookies that don't require turning on an oven, that can be whipped up by embellishing store-bought items like shortbread, crackers, and pound cake.

Some of the recipes here employ store-bought cookies and crackers as a base for fantastic treats. Exquisite results can be had by dipping all-butter Walkers Shortbread Fingers into chocolate and rolling them in nuts and toffee bits, or by dabbing some marmalade onto vanilla wafers and covering them with white chocolate. And though you may read "saltines" and then think "soup," I'm here to tell you that these humble crackers, when topped with buttery toffee, chocolate, and coconut, make unbelievably crave-inducing cookies.

Then there are simple recipes that look labored over:

Marshmallow and rice cereal treats can be cut into circles and frosted to approximate everyone's favorite black and white cookies. Bite-size squares of pound cake can be covered with softly hued icing and elegantly decorated to look like real petits fours.

If I have one guiding rule for swappable shortcut cookies, it is to use the same high-quality ingredients when beginning with a box of graham crackers or saltines as when baking from scratch. Use white chocolate with plenty of cocoa butter—at least 20 percent—when making White Chocolate and Marmalade Vanilla Wafers. Insist on all-butter frozen pound cake for Cheater's Petits Fours. Your friends and family will feel richly rewarded by your minimal but thoughtful efforts (and they don't need to know how easy it all was!).

Chocolate-Toffee Shortbread Fingers

Walkers Shortbread comes as close to a homemade cookie as anything you'll find in a supermarket aisle. It's made with the same pure ingredients—flour, butter, sugar, and salt—that you would use yourself. And when you dip these cookies in chocolate and coat them with nuts and toffee, well, you can imagine how tempting they are.

Sometimes you can find Walkers Shortbread discounted at the warehouse clubs or at Target. If you do, grab as many boxes as you can (Walkers says its shortbread will stay fresh, unopened, for more than a year). That way you'll be prepared for any cookie swap invitation that comes along.

MAKES: 48 cookies
QUICK PREP

½ **cup toasted and cooled pecans (see Note), coarsely chopped**

¾ **cup Heath Bits 'O Brickle Toffee bits or coarsely chopped SKOR or Heath bars**

1 bag (12 ounces) bittersweet or semisweet chocolate chips

1 tablespoon vegetable oil

4 packages (8.8-ounces each) Walkers Pure Butter Shortbread Fingers (48 cookies total)

1. Line a few baking sheets with parchment paper. Combine the nuts and toffee bits in a shallow bowl.

2. Combine the chocolate and oil in a small microwave-safe bowl. Heat the chocolate in the microwave on high until melted, 30 seconds to 1 minute depending on the strength of your microwave. Stir until smooth. (Alternatively, place water to a depth of 1 inch in the bottom of a double boiler or a large saucepan and bring to a bare simmer. Place the chocolate chips and oil in the top of the double boiler or in a stainless steel bowl big enough to rest on top of the saucepan without touching the water. Heat, whisking occasionally, until the chocolate is melted.)

3. Hold a cookie by one end and dip it into the chocolate, turning, to coat three quarters of the cookie; let the excess drip back into the bowl. Hold the cookie over the bowl of nuts and toffee bits and sprinkle some of the mixture onto the chocolate-coated top and sides of the cookie. Place the cookie on a prepared baking sheet. Repeat with the remaining cookies. Let the cookies rest until the chocolate is set, about 30 minutes.

Chocolate-Toffee Shortbread Fingers will keep, between layers of parchment paper, in an airtight container at room temperature for up to 1 week.

Note: To toast the pecans, place them in a single layer on an ungreased baking sheet and bake in a 350°F oven, shaking the pan occasionally, until fragrant, 5 to 10 minutes. Watch them closely to make sure they don't burn, and transfer the toasted nuts to a plate to let them cool.

White Chocolate and Marmalade Vanilla Wafers

These cookies dazzle but couldn't be simpler to make.

This is a lightning-fast way to make scrumptious little cookie bites. You simply dab marmalade onto a tray full of vanilla wafers and then cloak each cookie in melted white chocolate. For a fittingly elegant garnish, you can top each one with a tiny piece of candied orange peel (available in specialty food stores and by mail; see Resources, page 216).

MAKES: 48 cookies
QUICK PREP

48 vanilla wafer cookies, such as Nilla Wafers

½ cup orange marmalade

1 bag (12 ounces) white chocolate chips

Candied orange peel, for garnish (optional)

1. Place the vanilla wafer cookies, rounded sides down, on wire racks set on top of baking sheets. Place ½ teaspoon of marmalade on the flat side of each cookie.

2. Place the white chocolate chips in a microwave-safe bowl and microwave on high, stirring once or twice, until just melted, 1 to 2 minutes depending on the strength of your microwave. Stir until smooth. (Alternatively, place water to a depth of 1 inch in the bottom of a double boiler or a large saucepan

and bring to a bare simmer. Place the white chocolate chips in the top of the double boiler or in a stainless steel bowl big enough to rest on top of the saucepan without touching the water. Heat, whisking occasionally, until the chocolate is just melted. Remove from the heat and whisk until smooth.)

3. Use a small offset spatula to spread white chocolate over each cookie,

covering the marmalade and coming to the edges. Place the baking sheets in the refrigerator for 5 minutes to allow the chocolate to set.

White Chocolate and Marmalade Vanilla Wafers will keep, layered between parchment paper, at room temperature in an airtight container for up to 3 days.

 Party On

The Need for Speed // LOW-COMMITMENT COOKIE SWAP

There's no room for guilt in cookie swapdom. If you want to have an exchange but just don't feel up to baking from scratch, don't sweat it. Instead, invite people to a no-pressure swap and suggest recipes from this chapter. (Your beyond-busy friends can even get by with a box or two of high-quality bakery cookies—but just this once.)

Your snack menu can come from any local takeout joint. Or, if you want to theme it up, you could order Chinese food and set out inexpensive chopsticks, trays and baskets, and classic Chinese takeout boxes for packing up the cookies (all of these items can be purchased at Pearl River; see Resources, page 216).

Chocolate-Caramel Graham Cracker Sandwiches

Like a homemade Twix bar, but tastier!

Transform humble graham crackers into decadent candy bar–like treats by sandwiching them with homemade caramel (see "Smooth Talk," page 195, for prep tips) and coating them with a layer of chocolate. A sprinkling of gourmet sea salt is optional, but it's definitely worth a try—it balances the sweetness of the other ingredients and elevates the cookies to greater dessert heights. If you are really pressed for time, go ahead and use a jar of dulce de leche or other good-quality purchased caramel sauce for the filling instead of making your own.

MAKES: 48 cookies
QUICK PREP

¾ cup sugar

¼ cup heavy cream

¼ teaspoon salt

24 full graham cracker sheets, broken along perforations into 4 pieces each

1 bag (12 ounces) milk or semisweet chocolate chips

Maldon sea salt or other sea salt, for garnish (optional)

1. Line 2 rimmed baking sheets with parchment paper or aluminum foil.

2. Combine the sugar and ¼ cup of water in a small, heavy saucepan over

medium-high heat. Bring the mixture to a boil and cook, continuing to boil, until it becomes a light amber colored syrup, 5 to 7 minutes. (Do not stir the mixture while it cooks. If part of the syrup begins to darken more than the rest, gently tilt the pan to even out the cooking.)

3. When the syrup is a uniform amber color, stir in the heavy cream with a long-handled wooden spoon. Be careful, because the cream will bubble up. When the bubbling has subsided, stir in the salt. Transfer the sauce to a heat-proof bowl and let cool to warm room temperature.

4. Cover a work surface with sheets of wax paper. Use a small offset spatula to spread a little less than 1 teaspoon of the caramel sauce over one side of a graham cracker piece. Sandwich with another piece and set down on the work surface. Repeat with the remaining cookies. You should have 48 sandwich cookies in total.

5. Place the chocolate chips in a microwave-safe bowl and microwave on high until just melted, stirring

once or twice, 1½ to 3 minutes depending on the strength of your microwave. (Alternatively, place water to a depth of 1 inch in the bottom of a double boiler or a large saucepan and bring to a bare simmer. Place the chocolate chips in the top of the double boiler or in a stainless steel bowl big enough to rest on top of the saucepan without touching the water. Heat, whisking occasionally, until the chocolate is melted.)

6. Place a sandwich cookie in the bowl of melted chocolate and turn it with a fork to coat it lightly but completely. Use the fork to lift it from the bowl, letting any excess chocolate drip back into the bowl. Place the coated cookie on a prepared baking sheet. Repeat with the remaining cookies. Sprinkle the top of each with a little bit of sea salt if desired. Place the baking sheet in the refrigerator for 5 minutes to let the chocolate harden.

Chocolate-Caramel Graham Cracker Sandwiches will keep at room temperature in an airtight container for up to 1 week.

Coat the cookies in white chocolate if you prefer.

Smooth Talk FOOLPROOF CARAMEL PREP

Few recipes are as simple as the one for caramel. But making perfect caramel requires knowledge of how sugar cooks and some practice. Here are a few tips to help you get it right:

* Place the sugar in an even layer (don't pile it all up in the center) in a very clean, deep, heavy saucepan. A lighter pan might cause your caramel to burn in some spots before it cooks adequately in others.

* Add enough water to moisten the sugar, pouring it slowly into the pan so it doesn't splash sugar granules up and onto the sides of the pan. (Stray sugar crystals that haven't melted will hook up with melted sugar, creating a network of crystallized sugar that is grainy, rather than smooth.) A general guideline is 1 part water to 3 parts sugar; you want enough water to moisten the sugar, but not so much that it will take forever for the liquid to evaporate.

* Heat the pan over medium. Don't be tempted to rush and put the heat up all the way to high.

* To prevent crystallization, you can do a few things. As the caramel cooks, periodically wash down the sides of the pot with a wet pastry brush, encouraging all of the sugar crystals to melt. Or try this method: As soon as the sugar and water mixture begins to bubble, cover the pot for 1 minute and turn the heat to low. The steam trapped by the lid will drip down the sides of the pan, washing down any remaining crystals.

Alternatively, make dry caramel by heating the sugar without water in the pan. You'll have to watch the sugar carefully, because it cooks more quickly when it's dry, but there's no chance of crystallization because there's no water.

* Don't stir! The more you stir, the more you'll disturb the sugar molecules, encouraging them to link up into a lumpy, gritty mass. If your sugar is cooking unevenly, gently tilt the pan to even out the cooking, rotating it if necessary to slow down cooking in one spot while speeding it up elsewhere.

* Watch the caramel carefully and remove the pan from the heat as soon as it takes on a uniformly amber color. Any darker than this and it will have a distinctly burnt flavor.

* For easy pan cleanup, add some water to the messy pan and bring it to a boil. This will loosen the caramel from the pan, allowing you to wash it easily.

Saltine Toffee Bark

Crispy, crunchy, buttery, sweet, salty—and easy. What's not to love?

MAKES: 48 cookies
BAKE TIME: 5 minutes
QUICK PREP

Saltines? For dessert? Yes—and how good they are! Crackly crisp, drenched with buttery toffee, blanketed with chocolate, and then sprinkled with coconut and nuts . . . these salty-sweet cookies are absolutely addictive. And since they're made with a sleeve of saltine crackers and a few other pantry items, they couldn't be simpler to assemble. The cooled cookies easily break apart into 48 pieces—all the better to swap with!

Nonstick cooking spray

48 saltine crackers (1 sleeve)

1 cup (2 sticks) unsalted butter

1 cup packed dark brown sugar

1 bag (12 ounces) semisweet chocolate chips

1 cup unsweetened coconut

⅔ cup finely chopped pecans, almonds, or walnuts

1. Preheat the oven to 400°F. Line a rimmed 15 x 10 x 1 inch baking sheet (jelly roll pan) with heavy-duty aluminum foil and lightly spray the foil with nonstick cooking spray. Arrange the crackers on top of the foil in a single layer, so they are touching each other at the edges.

2. Combine the butter and sugar in a heavy saucepan and bring to a boil over medium-high heat, stirring occasionally. Turn the heat to low and simmer until the mixture is thick and golden, 3 minutes. Pour the mixture over the crackers and spread it to the edges of the pan with a rubber spatula.

3. Place the baking sheet in the oven and bake until the toffee is bubbling, 5 minutes. Transfer the baking sheet to a wire rack and sprinkle the chocolate chips over the toffee-covered crackers. As the chocolate chips melt, use the spatula to spread them into an even layer. Sprinkle the coconut and nuts over the chocolate. Let the cookies cool completely, then break them into 48 pieces.

Saltine Toffee Bark will keep, layered between parchment paper, in an airtight container at room temperature for up to 1 week.

"Forget love . . . I'd rather fall in chocolate!"

UNKNOWN

Cheater's Petits Fours

Decorate these diminutive sweets with any color glaze you choose.

MAKES: 36 little cakes
QUICK PREP

These little cakes are fun to make and decorate, especially since there's no baking involved. Leave lots of time, however, for icing them: They'll need to be covered with two layers to get a nice, shiny finish. But don't fret about the extra effort involved—you'll get to flex your creativity muscles, *and* you'll end up with an impressive swap table offering.

2 frozen all-butter pound cakes (10.75 ounces each), thawed

3 tablespoons seedless raspberry jam (or another flavor of your choice)

⅔ cup light corn syrup

½ cup hot water

7 cups confectioners' sugar

2 teaspoons pure almond extract

Food coloring

Edible glitter or small sugar decorations

1. Line two rimmed baking sheets with aluminum foil and set wire racks on top.

2. On a work surface, use a sharp, serrated knife to trim the ends off of each cake. Slice each cake widthwise into six 1-inch slices. Trim the domed top portion away from each slice. Cut each slice into six 1-inch cubes, then halve the cubes.

3. Spread ¼ teaspoon jam over the cut side of the bottom half of each cube and sandwich with the top half. Place the jam-filled cake sandwiches least 1 inch apart on the wire racks.

4. Whisk together the corn syrup and hot water in a small bowl. Whisk in the confectioners' sugar until smooth. Whisk in the almond extract.

5. Divide the icing among three or four small bowls and color each with food coloring as desired. Use a spoon to pour the icing over each petit four, covering it completely with the icing. Let stand until set, about 15 minutes, and then repeat, to give each one a nice coating (if the icing becomes stiff, just re-whisk it until it is pourable and smooth). Top each petit four with a sprinkling of edible glitter and/or a small sugar decoration and let stand until the icing is completely set, about 1 hour.

Cheater's Petits Fours will keep, layered between parchment paper, in an airtight container at room temperature for up to 3 days.

The word cookie *comes from the Dutch "koekje," and literally means "little cake." Cookies arrived in America with the first European settlers in the 1600s.*

WHEREFORE ART THOU, PETITS FOURS? A BRIEF HISTORY

Petit four literally means "small oven" in French. In the eighteenth century, people conserved their precious coal by baking large cakes and bread first, and then using the still-warm oven to bake small cakes and other confections. These little pastries came to be known as petits fours, and as years passed they evolved into elaborate cakes in miniature, decorated in imitation of their full-size cousins. Eventually, many types of small treats—bonbons, pralines, marzipan candies—were placed under the petit four umbrella. But for many people, the words "petit four" still bring the iconic tiny, iced cake to mind.

Marshmallow Treat
Black-and-Whites

Black-and-white cookies are a perennial favorite, probably because they please vanilla and chocolate fans alike (and ease the angst for those of us who just can't decide!). Now even non-bakers can make everyone happy with this spin on the beloved bakery classic: Simply cut a sheet of marshmallow treats into circles, and frost them with two icings.

FOR THE MARSHMALLOW TREATS

Nonstick cooking spray

3 tablespoons unsalted butter

1 package (10.5 ounces) mini marshmallows

½ teaspoon pure vanilla extract

¼ teaspoon salt

4 cups puffed rice cereal

FOR THE "VANILLA" ICING

1⅓ cups confectioners' sugar

¼ cup heavy cream, plus more as needed

1 teaspoon fresh lemon juice

FOR THE CHOCOLATE ICING

4 ounces bittersweet chocolate, finely chopped

¼ cup heavy cream

1 tablespoon plus 1 teaspoon light corn syrup

½ teaspoon pure vanilla extract

1. Make the marshmallow treats: Line a baking sheet with heavy-duty aluminum foil and spray it with nonstick cooking spray. Spray a large offset spatula as well. Line a few baking sheets with wax paper and set aside.

2. Melt the butter in a large saucepan over low heat. Add the marshmallows, vanilla, and salt and stir with a rubber spatula until smooth. Remove the pan from the heat and stir in the rice cereal to coat it.

3. Turn the mixture out onto the foil-lined baking sheet and use the prepared offset spatula to spread it into a thin layer. You won't be able to cover the whole sheet, but you should be able to get it into a 12-inch square. Let cool completely.

4. When the large marshmallow treat is cooled, lift it, still on the foil, from the baking sheet and transfer it to a cutting board. Use a 2-inch round cutter to cut it into 36 circles. Transfer the circles to the wax-paper–lined baking sheets.

5. Make the "vanilla" icing: Whisk together the confectioners' sugar, cream, and lemon juice in a small bowl until smooth, whisking in additional cream, one teaspoon at a time, if necessary to make a spreadable (but not runny) icing. With a small metal spatula, spread the icing on one half of each treat. Let stand 15 minutes to set.

6. Make the chocolate icing: Combine the chocolate, cream, and corn syrup in a microwave-safe bowl and microwave on high until the chocolate is just melted, 30 seconds to 1 minute depending on the strength of your microwave. Whisk until smooth. Whisk in the vanilla. (Alternatively, place water to a depth of 1 inch in the bottom of a double boiler or a large saucepan and bring to a bare simmer. Place the chocolate, cream, corn syrup, and vanilla in the top of the double boiler or in a stainless steel bowl big enough to rest on top of the saucepan without touching the water. Heat, whisking occasionally, until the chocolate is melted.) If necessary, let the icing stand for a few minutes until it is thick enough to spread. You should be able to smooth it easily over the cookies, but it shouldn't be so loose that it runs down the sides.

7. Spread the chocolate icing on the other half of each treat. Let stand until both icings are fully set, at least 1 hour.

Marshmallow Treat Black-and-Whites will keep, layered between wax paper, at room temperature for up to 5 days.

To make this recipe even easier, you can use store-bought icings instead of homemade.

No-Bake Chocolate Bourbon Bites

Kids can't resist cookies, so keep these boozy bites out of reach!

MAKES: 48 bites
QUICK PREP

This no-bake treat is a cross between a cookie and a bonbon. Walkers Shortbread gives the cookies a buttery richness, but for a slightly sweeter, lighter taste you can substitute 10 ounces of vanilla wafers (that's slightly less than one 12-ounce box, about 70 little cookies). Dark rum also works well in place of the bourbon, but no matter what type of liquor you choose, invest in a bottle of the good stuff.

¾ cup sugar, plus extra for rolling the cookies

16 Walkers Shortbread cookies (from two 5.3-ounce boxes)

1 cup pecans

1 cup semisweet chocolate chips

3 tablespoons light corn syrup

½ cup Kentucky bourbon

1. Line several baking sheets with parchment paper.

2. Place ¼ cup of the sugar in a shallow bowl and set aside. Combine the cookies and pecans in a food processor and pulse 7 to 10 times until finely ground (the mixture should resemble coarse sand). Transfer to a large mixing bowl.

3. Place the chocolate chips in a microwave-safe bowl and microwave on high until just melted, 1 to 2 minutes. Whisk until smooth. (Alternatively, place water to a depth of 1 inch in the bottom of a double boiler or a large saucepan and bring to a bare simmer. Place the chocolate chips in the top of the double boiler or in a stainless steel bowl big enough to rest on top of the saucepan without touching the water. Heat, whisking occasionally, until the chocolate is melted.) Whisk in the remaining ½ cup of sugar, the corn syrup, and the bourbon. Stir in the cookie mixture.

4. Working over the the bowl, roll heaping teaspoons of the cookie mixture between your palms. Set the balls on the prepared baking sheets and place in the freezer until firm, 5 to 10 minutes.

5. Remove the bourbon balls from the freezer and roll them in the sugar to coat. Place them back on the baking sheet, drape them lightly with plastic wrap, and refrigerate them until well chilled, about 3 hours.

No-Bake Chocolate Bourbon Bites will keep in an airtight container in the refrigerator for up to 1 week.

"There are four basic food groups: milk chocolate, dark chocolate, white chocolate, and chocolate truffles."

UNKNOWN

BLUE-RIBBON BOUNTY AWARD-WORTHY SWAG

Sure, the hallmark of a successful swap is a bounty of gorgeous cookies. But it's also great loot. Show your guests you care by handing out prizes to acknowledge their efforts. And avoid cookie monsters: Have prizes on hand for each guest. Every cookie will have its merits, so don't be afraid to go wild with the awards. Cookie cutters, cookie scoops, mini baking spatulas, aprons, small trophies, ribbons, sashes, and medals are all fun (see Resources, page 216, for sources). Prize categories might include: Most Beautiful, Most Original, Most Popular, Spiciest, Richest, Most Chocolaty, Most Allergen-Friendly, and Nuttiest (as in packed with the most nuts . . . or weirdest).

BEYOND MILK

PERFECT SWAP SIPS

I t would be possible, I suppose, to plan a cookie exchange that is all business. With no preliminaries, the process would take a matter of minutes. Guests would arrive, pick up what they came for, and depart with a wave and a smile. But a cookie swap is as much about catching up with old friends and meeting new people as it is about the cookies. The proffering of drinks and snacks, however simple, will make your exchange a real, bonafide cookie bash.

What you serve at your swap will depend on the occasion, crowd, time of day, time of year, and time you have to prepare. Go ahead, don't be shy—feel free to ask everyone to bring an extra half-dozen cookies to be served at the party (for more on this, see pages 5–7). Once that's settled, your only obligation is to provide plates, napkins, and an array of drinks, arrange the cookies on a table or countertop, and let the munching begin.

You may decide that you want to do more, perhaps save the sweets for later and set out some savories for your guests to enjoy before the swapping gets underway. In this case, choosing a "signature" drink can help inspire the rest of your menu. I wrote this chapter with that thought in mind, and came up with a bunch of beverages that beg to be served with, before, or after cookies. They're easy to make in quantity and, most important, they're fun to drink.

Alongside these recipes you'll find ideas for simple but festive food to match. As I remarked way back in Chapter 1, I'm all about prepping food ahead of time whenever possible to alleviate any party-day stress. The menu suggestions I offer here involve relatively simple foods that require little in the way of effort. Still, to make the planning and prep stages easier, I urge you to buy, assemble, and cook whatever you can in advance, so you have to worry only about reheating and/or plating on swap day.

Hot Chocolate
for a Crowd

The double whammy of bittersweet chocolate and cocoa powder makes this hot chocolate extra rich. As the recipe title suggests, this makes enough for a crowd of twelve but feel free to double the recipe if you expect more revelers. Most cookies pair well with hot chocolate, but cookies with ground nuts and/or a strong flavor of vanilla (Pistachio Sacristans, page 83; Mini Hazelnut Linzer Hearts, page 118; Very Vanilla Sprinkle Cookies, page 49; Vanilla Pretzels, page 132) are especially good choices for serving alongside. *Serves 12.*

8 cups whole milk

12 ounces bittersweet chocolate, finely chopped (about 2 cups)

2 tablespoons unsweetened cocoa powder (natural or Dutch-process will work)

1 teaspoon pure vanilla extract

1. Place the milk in a large saucepan over medium-high heat and bring it just to a boil (watch it closely—you don't want it to boil in earnest or it will curdle). Reduce the heat to low and whisk in the chocolate and cocoa powder. Continue to whisk until the chocolate is melted and the mixture is smooth, 2 to 4 minutes.

I WANT CANDY

If you are a bona fide sweet freak and a cookie swap alone won't satisfy your cravings, up the sugar factor by assembling a candy buffet. Get some large clear plastic containers (look for inexpensive ones at IKEA or Pier 1 Imports) and fill each one to the brim with candy (see Resources, page 216). Put out little bowls or bags and let people mix and match as they please.

Christmas: Peppermints, red licorice wheels or nibs, gummy spearmint leaves, red and green M&M's

Kwanzaa: Black licorice laces, black jelly beans, gummy raspberries, red Swedish fish, green-foil-wrapped Hershey Kisses, Sour Patch Apples

Hanukkah: Blue jelly beans, blue raspberry gummy sharks, gold-foil-wrapped coins (Hanukkah gelt), gold-foil-wrapped Jordan almonds

Valentine's Day: Conversation Hearts; Hershey's Kisses; cinnamon Red Hots; pink and white M&M's; pink, red, and white jelly beans

Easter: Peeps, pastel-colored jelly beans, Cadbury Cream Eggs, malted milk eggs, pastel-colored M&M's

Halloween: Black licorice whips, gummy worms, wax fangs/lips, orange jelly beans, ghost- or cat-shaped Peeps

2. Remove the pan from the heat and stir in the vanilla. (The hot cocoa can be stored in the fridge at this point; see "A Step Ahead," left.) Pour the hot cocoa into mugs and serve it immediately, or transfer it to a thermal carafe and serve as needed.

VARIATIONS
Richest Hot Chocolate
Substitute 2 cups of heavy cream for 2 cups of the milk.

Peppermint Hot Chocolate
Substitute ½ teaspoon pure peppermint extract for the vanilla extract.

Iced
Irish Coffee

For an alcohol-free version, use milk in place of the whiskey.

This chilled, boozy confection is like a creamy coffee ice-cream float. It's a refreshing summertime alternative to the traditional hot drink. For the best flavor and consistency, use the finest coffee, whiskey, and ice cream you can find. Nibble on Incredibly Fudgy Brownies (page 55) as you sip your frozen coffee. Pure heaven. *Serves 8.*

8 cups strong, brewed coffee

2 tablespoons superfine sugar

1 pint coffee ice cream

½ cup Irish whiskey

Combine the coffee and sugar in a pitcher and whisk to dissolve the sugar. Refrigerate until well chilled. Place ¼ cup of coffee ice cream in the bottom of each of 8 tall glasses. Pour the chilled coffee and whiskey into each glass and serve with long-handled spoons.

VARIATIONS

Substitute Kahlua, sambuca, or ouzo for the whiskey to make Iced Mexican, Roman, or Greek coffee.

Mulled Cider

Set a pot of cider on the stove to perfume the house before your guests arrive.

Mulled cider is delicious on a cold day, and is a great match for the casual party food people crave when the chill sets in. As an added benefit, it perfumes your home with its wonderful aroma. If you'd like to give your guests the choice of alcoholic or nonalcoholic cider, just leave a bottle of Calvados (apple brandy) alongside your pot and let them serve themselves. The perfect cookie pairing? You won't do any better than Classic Oatmeal Raisin Cookies (page 45), in my opinion. But any cookies with warm spices, such as cinnamon and cardamom, would be excellent bedfellows. *Serves 8.*

¼ cup packed light brown sugar

Pinch of salt

Pinch of nutmeg

½ teaspoon whole cloves

½ cinnamon stick

1 quart apple cider

⅔ cup Calvados (optional)

Combine the sugar, salt, nutmeg, cloves, cinnamon stick, and cider in a large saucepan and bring to a boil over medium-high heat. Reduce the heat, cover, and simmer for 20 minutes. Stir in the Calvados if desired, then ladle into mugs, and serve.

MENU

Autumn Nibbles

Baby, it's cold out there! Ward off the chill at your next autumnal swap with cups of mulled cider and some of these rich, seasonal bites:

* *Grilled cheddar cheese and grainy mustard sandwiches*

* *Roasted cumin-and-chili-powder-spiced pumpkin seeds*

* *Figs stuffed with goat cheese and prosciutto and baked (in a 350°F oven until warm, about 10 minutes)*

* *Baked prepared puff pastry topped with crumbled bacon, sautéed onions, and fresh arugula*

MENU
Lemonade Stand Lunch

Fêtes on hot summer days call out for icy lemonade and some cooling salads like these:

* Asian chicken salad with snow peas, water chestnuts, and chow mein noodles, dressed with bottled ginger dressing

* Chopped shrimp, celery, and avocado, dressed with olive oil and lemon juice

* Traditional egg salad with shallots and capers

* Cubed watermelon and feta cheese, sprinkled with mint and drizzled with lime juice

* Baby greens salad with lightly steamed chopped summer veggies

Old-Fashioned Lemonade

A must-serve at any warm-weather swap.

To give this lemonade some kick, stir 1 cup of gin into the pitcher before pouring it over ice. *Serves 10.*

3 cups strained fresh lemon juice

1 cup superfine sugar

Ice, for serving

1. Combine the lemon juice with 6 cups of water and the sugar in a large mixing bowl and whisk to dissolve the sugar. Pour the lemonade into a large pitcher and refrigerate until well chilled, at least 3 hours (or up to 2 days).

2. Pour the lemonade into tall glasses over ice just before serving.

VARIATION
Mint and Ginger Lemonade

Combine 1 cup of packed, washed fresh mint leaves and ¼ cup of finely chopped fresh ginger (no need to peel it) in a heat-proof bowl. Boil 2 cups of the water, pour it over the mint and ginger, and let it stand for 30 minutes. Pour the mixture through a fine strainer and into a large bowl. Stir in the lemon juice, remaining 4 cups of water, and sugar and proceed as directed.

Mini Strawberry Milk Shakes

The fresh strawberries in these mini shakes elevate them from the soda fountain standard (yes, it *is* possible). Serve these in small glasses along with Old-Fashioned Lemonade (opposite) at a warm-weather cookie soiree. *Serves 8.*

1 pound fresh strawberries, washed, stemmed, and sliced

¼ cup sugar

1 teaspoon pure vanilla extract

2 pints vanilla ice cream, softened

1 cup whole milk

1. Combine the strawberries, sugar, and vanilla in a medium bowl and let stand, stirring occasionally, until the sugar is dissolved, about 15 minutes.

2. Place half of the strawberries and half of their liquid in a blender with 1 pint ice cream and ½ cup milk. Blend until smooth and pour into small glasses. Repeat with the remaining strawberries, strawberry liquid, ice cream, and milk. Serve immediately.

Real Southern Sweet Tea

Love Southern-style sweet tea? Here's the secret: Add a pinch of baking soda to temper the tea's bitterness. Just as baking soda neutralizes acids in cookie doughs made with nonalkalized cocoa powder, yogurt, and other acidic ingredients, it tames the acidity and bitterness in tea, making it smooth and thirst-quenching, without that tannic, mouth-drying kick. *Serves 10.*

6 tea bags (I use Lipton)

¼ teaspoon baking soda

1 cup superfine sugar or more to taste

Ice, for serving

Place the tea bags and baking soda in a heat-proof gallon pitcher. Bring 6 cups of water to a boil and pour over the tea bags. Set the pitcher aside to brew and cool for 1 hour. Remove the tea bags and stir in the sugar until dissolved. Add 3 cups of room-temperature water.

Refrigerate until chilled. Pour the tea into tall glasses over ice and garnish with lemon slices just before serving.

VARIATION
Arnold Palmers

To make a couple of pitchers of Arnold Palmers (a classic drink that's equal parts iced tea and lemonade), combine a recipe of Old-Fashioned Lemonade (page 210) with a recipe of Real Southern Sweet Tea. Pour into tall glasses over ice.

Fresh Lime Margaritas

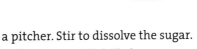

Freshly squeezed juice makes all the difference when making margaritas. Top-shelf tequila doesn't hurt, either! *Serves 8.*

2 cups good-quality tequila

1 cup Cointreau or triple sec

2½ cups fresh lime juice

1¼ cups fresh orange juice

½ cup superfine sugar

½ cup kosher salt

Lime wedges

Crushed ice, for serving

1. Combine the tequila, Cointreau, lime juice, orange juice, and sugar in a pitcher. Stir to dissolve the sugar. Refrigerate until chilled.

2. Spread the salt in an even layer on a small plate. Rub the lime wedges around the rims of 8 margarita or martini glasses to moisten. Dip the rims in the salt. Fill each glass with crushed ice. Pour the margarita mixture into each glass and serve immediately.

MENU

Spicy Snacks for Drinks with a Kick

Pouring potent margaritas at your party? You'll want to serve some assertive appetizers that can hold their own.

- Pepper jack quesadillas

- Black-bean-and-mango salsa with chips

- Jicama sprinkled with lime juice, salt, and chili powder

- Mini corn muffins spiked with fresh corn, Cheddar cheese, and jalapeño

- Chilled shrimp and cocktail sauce kicked up with Tabasco Chipotle Pepper sauce

- Blue and white tortilla chips with salsa and guacamole

MENU

Simple Tapas

Spanish-style bar food goes well with juicy sangria. Choose from the following for an easy cocktail buffet. Olé!

* Mixed olives

* Marcona almonds

* Manchego cheese with fig or apricot jam on crostini

* Cold Spanish omelet wedges

* Serrano ham wrapped around steamed asparagus

* Broiled or grilled chorizo-and-shrimp skewers

* Cheese straws

Juicy Sangria

Citrus fruits, apples, grapes, pitted cherries . . . toss any of your favorite fruits into the pitcher.

Making sangria is a festive and economical way to serve wine at a party. The best mixes are fresh and natural tasting, so avoid recipes that include ginger ale or lemon-lime soda—they're too sweet. Club soda is all that's needed to give the punch some fizz. *Serves 8 to 10.*

1 bottle dry red wine, such as Rioja, chilled

¼ cup Cointreau or triple sec

1 cup fresh orange juice

¼ cup fresh lemon juice

2 tablespoons superfine sugar or more to taste

Ice, for serving

4 cups chilled club soda, for serving

1 orange, thinly sliced, for serving

1 lemon, thinly sliced, for serving

1. Combine the wine, Cointreau, orange juice, lemon juice, and sugar in a large pitcher and stir to dissolve the sugar. Refrigerate for up to 6 hours.

2. Just before serving, pour the mixture into a punch bowl. Add ice cubes, club soda, and fruit slices.

Conversion Tables

LIQUID CONVERSIONS

U.S.	IMPERIAL	METRIC
2 tbs	1 fl oz	30 ml
3 tbs	1½ fl oz	45 ml
¼ cup	2 fl oz	60 ml
⅓ cup	2½ fl oz	75 ml
⅓ cup + 1 tbs	3 fl oz	90 ml
⅓ cup + 2 tbs	3½ fl oz	100 ml
½ cup	4 fl oz	125 ml
⅔ cup	5 fl oz	150 ml
¾ cup	6 fl oz	175 ml
¾ cup + 2 tbs	7 fl oz	200 ml
1 cup	8 fl oz	250 ml
1 cup + 2 tbs	9 fl oz	275 ml
1¼ cups	10 fl oz	300 ml
1⅓ cups	11 fl oz	325 ml
1½ cups	12 fl oz	350 ml
1⅔ cups	13 fl oz	375 ml
1¾ cups	14 fl oz	400 ml
1¾ cups + 2 tbs	15 fl oz	450 ml
2 cups (1 pint)	16 fl oz	500 ml
2½ cups	20 fl oz (1 pint)	600 ml
3¾ cups	1½ pints	900 ml
4 cups	1¾ pints	1 liter

WEIGHT CONVERSIONS

US/UK	METRIC	US/UK	METRIC
½ oz	15 g	7 oz	200 g
1 oz	30 g	8 oz	250 g
1½ oz	45 g	9 oz	275 g
2 oz	60 g	10 oz	300 g
2½ oz	75 g	11 oz	325 g
3 oz	90 g	12 oz	350 g
3½ oz	100 g	13 oz	375 g
4 oz	125 g	14 oz	400 g
5 oz	150 g	15 oz	450 g
6 oz	175 g	1 lb	500 g

OVEN TEMPERATURES

FAHRENHEIT	GAS MARK	CELSIUS
250	½	120
275	1	140
300	2	150
325	3	160
350	4	180
375	5	190
400	6	200
425	7	220
450	8	230
475	9	240
500	10	260

Note: *Reduce the temperature by 20°C (68°F) for fan-assisted ovens.*

APPROXIMATE EQUIVALENTS

1 stick butter = 8 tbs = 4 oz = ½ cup

1 cup all-purpose presifted flour or dried bread crumbs = 5 oz

1 cup granulated sugar = 8 oz

1 cup (packed) brown sugar = 6 oz

1 cup confectioners' sugar = 4½ oz

1 cup honey or syrup = 12 oz

1 cup grated cheese = 4 oz

1 cup dried beans = 6 oz

1 large egg = about 2 oz or about 3 tbs

1 egg yolk = about 1 tbs

1 egg white = about 2 tbs

Please note that all conversions are approximate but close enough to be useful when converting from one system to another.

Resources

In olden days, when I had to run from store to store looking for just the right cheetah-print bandannas to line my baskets, meringue powder for my icing, and animal-shaped cookie cutters to give out as party favors, shopping for a cookie swap was a lot of work. But now that virtually any item I can dream of is just a few mouse clicks away, shopping for any kind of party is a lot less stressful and a lot more fun. Here is a list of the online and mail-order sources I use frequently to simplify my baking and make my gatherings memorable.

BAKING STUFF

CandyFavorites.com
1101 Fifth Ave
McKeesport, PA 15132
1-888-525-7577
www.candyfavorites.com

My favorite online candy store. There are so many ways to shop for a candy buffet here: Search heart-shaped candy for Valentine's Day or a wedding shower, Christmas candy for a holiday buffet, or by decades for retro candies (great for a birthday). Or search candy by color if you want to set out a blue-and-gold selection for Hanukkah or orange-and-black for Halloween.

CopperGifts
900 North 32nd St.
Parsons, KS 67357
1-620-421-0654
www.coppergifts.com

This Kansas-based family business sells more than 1,000 different copper cookie cutters. I'm addicted. I've recently added a squirrel, a running gingerbread man, a poodle, and the State of New York to my collection. I just sent Vermont to my sister-in-law. If they don't have the shape you want, they will custom-craft a cutter just for you in a few days. CopperGifts also sells a wide range of cookie-decorating supplies, including nonpareils, edible glitter, and luster dust.

King Arthur Flour
The Baker's Catalogue
58 Billings Farm Road
White River Junction, VT 05001
1-800-827-6836
www.kingarthurflour.com

This catalog and online shop is the only place you'll need to go for high-quality cookie-baking equipment: baking sheets, wire racks, bulk parchment paper, spatulas, cookie scoops, pastry bags and tips, and KitchenAid mixers at competitive prices. Also check out their baking ingredients:

meringue powder, gel food coloring, sanding sugar, sprinkles, bittersweet chocolate chips, dried cherries, and a variety of flours. You can also visit their flagship location, The Baker's Store & Café, in Norwich, VT.

N.Y. Cake & Baking Distributor

56 West 22nd St.
New York, NY 10021
1-877-692-2538
www.nycake.com

This purveyor features lots of useful cookie baking supplies, including equipment like stencils, parchment paper, spatulas, and holiday-themed cookie cutters (as well as ½-inch heart-shaped aspic cutters, helpful for making the windows in Mini Hazelnut Linzer Hearts, page 118). They also carry an array of decorations, such as sprinkles, food coloring gels and pens, luster dust, and edible glitter. In addition to an online store, there are physical locations in New York (their flagship store, listed above) and Los Angeles.

Sur La Table

P.O. Box 840
Brownsburg, IN 46112
1-800-243-0852
www.surlatable.com

A good source for high-end bakeware, cookie cutter sets, and instant-read thermometers in rainbow shades (clever party favors). Sur La Table stores can be found throughout the United States.

PARTY STUFF

BRP Box Shop

823 South Third Street
Clinton, IA 52732
1-563-243-5210
www.brpboxshop.com

If your local bakery won't sell you cardboard bakery boxes, you can mail order them from this website. Choose from natural brown, white, and many other colors. They also sell boxes with heart, star, Christmas tree, shamrock, and teddy bear cutouts on top, smart choices for themed cookie swaps.

Cookietins.com

P.O. Box 1351
Belaire, TX 77402-1351
1-832-518-2800
www.e-cookietins.com

Having trouble tracking down a decent cookie tin? This website sells attractive tins in a variety of shapes and sizes at very reasonable prices.

E-Favors.com

362 41st Street, BA
Brooklyn, NY 11232
1-800-455-9965
www.efavors.com

A one-stop shop for inexpensive party favors. Take a look at the personalized mini glass cookie jars (at the time of this writing, $1.70 each) and "A Star Is Born" cookie cutter set, tied with a ribbon (irresistible for a baby shower—and also inexpensive).

Fortune Cookie Soap

P.O. Box 594
Jenks, OK 74037
1-888-347-6802
www.fortunecookiesoap.com

The name says it all—this
is an entire Web catalog
devoted to handmade soap in
the shape of fortune cookies,
each one with a fortune
inside. For about four dollars
each, these make unique
favors and gifts.

Lucky Clover Trading

4950 E. Second St.
Benicia, CA 94510
1-800-338-5825
www.luckyclovertrading.com

When you're short on
serving pieces for your swap
table, check out this site for
unbelievably inexpensive
baskets and trays.

Oriental Trading

P.O. Box 2308
Omaha, NE 68103-2308
1-800-875-8480
www.orientaltrading.com

If you've thrown a party
recently, you've probably
gotten wind of this online
retailer. This standby of school
moms everywhere is a reliable
place to go for gift bags,
bandannas (for lining cookie
baskets), piñatas, and paper
and plastic goods. There's a lot
of junk here, but if you pick
and choose carefully, you can
pull together a terrific party—
including decorations, favors,
and tableware—for a great
price.

Party City

www.partycity.com

A one-stop shop (with
locations nationwide) for
all your party needs, with
some clever offerings for
theme parties (and even
costumes—if you want to
go that far).

Pearl River Mart

477 Broadway
New York, NY 10012
1-800-878-2446
www.pearlriver.com

At this Chinese American
department store (and their
online outpost), you can find
all sorts of party decorations
and tabletop items for your
swap. I'm a fan of their paper
garlands, table runners, and
ceramic platters. Their colorful
toys make quirky party favors.

Perpetual Kid

45965 Nokes Blvd., #180
Sterling, VA 20166
1-888-282-7115
www.perpetualkid.com

This online novelty store sells
lots of goofy stuff, but their
chocolate chip cookie soaps
and Oreo-shape key caps
(cleverly called Cookeys—get
it?) are especially "sweet."

RibbonQueen.com

P.O. Box 2642
Granite Bay, CA 95746
www.ribbonqueen.com

Buy beautiful and inexpensive
ribbon for packaging party
favors and cookie boxes from
this website. Take a look at
their old-fashioned gingham

and grosgrain, as well as their novelty prints, including fruits, animal prints, stars, and hearts.

Ribbons Galore

1780 Vernon St. #3
Roseville, CA 95678
1-800-919-9200
www.ribbonsgalore.com

Ever wondered where beauty queens get their sashes? This is the place. Personalized ribbons make unique party game prizes and can be bestowed upon winners of your "most creative" and "most popular" cookie contests. You can order from Ribbons Galore online, or from their bricks-and-mortar shop in California.

Shutterfly

2800 Bridge Parkway
Redwood City, CA 94065
1-888-225-7159
www.shutterfly.com

This is my favorite online digital photo service, reliable and easy to use. I've ordered custom photo invitations as well as cookie swap recipe booklets using their digital scrapbook application.

Sierra Mountain Candles

4742 Woodthrush Ln.
Sparks, NV 89436
1-775-626-9494
www.sierramtncandles.com

When you want the favors to be as decadent as the party, consider this company's cookie-scented candles, which come in a variety of flavors including biscotti, hot fudge brownie, oatmeal raisin, snickerdoodle, and chocolate chip.

Acknowledgments

hanks to Suzanne Rafer for thinking of me, baking away in my kitchen all the way out here on eastern Long Island, when putting together this wonderful project. And countless thank-yous to Kylie Foxx McDonald for transforming my manuscript into a scrumptious guide to all things swappable. May your creativity, care, and tremendous effort be rewarded with a lifetime supply of Flaky Pastry Pinwheels and Chocolate Shortbread Dominoes. Credit for excellent copyediting must go to Susan Casel, and for creative editorial assistance, thanks to Liz Davis. My gratitude goes to production editor Beth Levy for her unerring attention to detail. For designing a book that makes me want to bake, thanks to Rae Ann Spitzenberger; for setting it beautifully, thanks to Barbara Peragine. For capturing the joy of baking in wonderful photographs, thanks to Ben Fink. I am grateful to Cynthia Garcia-Vegas, Jose Martin Vegas, Anne Kerman, Janet Vicario, and Jen Browning for making these cookies look their best during their time in the spotlight. Thanks to Cathy Dorsey for a thorough, user-friendly index. Selina Meere has worked tirelessly to spread the word far and wide about the joy of cookie swapping. Thanks to Angela Miller for being my agent for all of these years; I think you were as excited about this book as I was. Friends, neighbors, and relatives, including Andrea Ackerman, Sue Bachemin, Harry Fischman, Jane Gill, Ellen Johansen, Dan Leader, Hal McKusick, Cheryl Merser, Roland Mesnier, Gail Pickering, Nancy Silverman, and Jake Wilson, have all cheerfully tasted whatever has come out of my oven. Thank you for letting my cookies into your homes. Friends of Rose and Eve (you know who you are!)—I appreciate your support in the cafeteria and on Facebook! And thanks a million times to my husband, Jack Bishop, who has once again sacrificed his cholesterol count for the sake of my baking career.

Index